JN114867

WORKBOOK
FOR
A SYSTEMATIC
APPROACH
TO
ENGLISH WORDS
Basic
5th Edition

by

YASUSHI SHIMO

MASAHIKO TONE

SUNDAI BUNKO

はしがき

　英単語を覚えるためには，目で読み，口に出し，耳で聞き，手で書くということを繰り返すしかありません。目だけで覚えることも，耳だけで覚えることも可能でしょうが，ほとんどの人は五感をバランスよく使って覚える方が効率よく覚えられるはずです。

　本書は『システム英単語 Basic 〈5訂版〉』に準拠し，書きこみ式で英語を覚えるワークブックです。『システム英単語 Basic 〈5訂版〉』の <minimal phrase> を確認し，全ての単語を3回書きこめるように作られています。つまり，覚えるために「書く」という動作を繰り返すために作られた本です。当たり前のことですが，書いたことのないことを書くのはとても難しいし，書いたことがあれば書けるようになります。書くという行為を反復すれば，「書ける」ようになります。本書を手にされた方は，今日から「書く」ことを始めて，「書ける」ようになってください。

☆「システム英単語」シリーズの英単語学習システム

　人間の脳は，一度覚えたことも，そのまま放っておけばその 70％を忘れてしまうと言われています。ですからどうやって効果的に再確認するかが極めて重要なのです。『システム英単語 Basic 〈5訂版〉』シリーズを使って，英単語を覚え，記憶を保つためのステップを下に挙げます。もちろん，人によって時間のかけ方は違っていいですし，場合によっては順番を反対にしてもいいのですが，ひとつの典型的なモデルだと思ってください。

　なお，本書は 30 単語を1セクションとしていますが，もちろん2セクション，3セクションを一気に扱ってもかまいません。自分の学習時間に合わせて進めてください。また，1日でどの Step まで進めるかも自分のペースで決めてください。たとえば同じ1セクション 30 個の単語を，1日に 1 Step ずつ5日間かけて進めてもよいですし，1日目に 1st Step，2nd Step と進めておき，2日目に 3rd Step，3日目に 4th Step，4日目に 5th Step へ進む，というのでもよいでしょう。要は自分のリズムに合わせればよいのです。

1st Step ＜単語と出会う＞

『システム英単語 Basic 〈5訂版〉』（別売）を読んで，単語の意味，語法などを確認。
ゆっくりでよいので，納得いくまで書籍を読んでください。納得いかないことは覚えられません。
納得できたら，フレーズを声に出して読んでみてください。

↓

2nd Step ＜耳と口で覚える＞

『システム英単語 Basic 〈5訂版〉CD』『同　音声ダウンロード』（別売）を聞きながら，声に出して覚える。
CD には英語フレーズが3回収録されていますから，覚えるのに最適です。
シャドウイングと言って，聞こえてくる英語とほぼ同時に口に出すと効果的です。
発音が下手でも大丈夫。とにかく大きな声で，何度も口に出すのが大事です。

↓

3rd Step ＜書いて覚える＞

『フレーズ・単語書きこみワークブック』（本書）でフレーズ・単語を 3 回書く。
書くときは集中して書きましょう。覚えたい，という気持ちが大事です。書き足りないと感じた場合は，納得いくまで何度でも書いてください（本書の書きこみ欄は3回分しかありませんが，「本書の使い方」にあるやり方で，何度でも使い込んでください）。たくさん書くから，書けるようになるのです。

↓

4th Step ＜単語を使う＞

『システム英単語 Basic〈5訂版対応〉チェック問題集』（別売）でチェックテスト。

一度覚えた英単語を「使う」ことは，長期記憶に有効です。チェックテストをして，自分の力で

「思い出そう」と考えることが重要なのです。能動的に使える単語（発表語彙）となれば，

長期間記憶に定着するようになります。できなかった単語は『システム英単語 Basic〈5訂版〉』で

しっかり確認しましょう。

↓

5th Step ＜覚えていることも再確認＞

『システム英単語 Basic〈5訂版〉CD』『同　音声ダウンロード』のシャドウイングで再確認。

『システム英単語 Basic〈5訂版〉』の記事を再確認し，もう一度本書のフレーズをチェック

してください（そのために本書の各ページ上部にある日付欄は3つあるのです）。

覚えているうちに再確認，これが長期記憶を作るのです。

　これでかなりの単語が記憶に残るはずです。もちろん中には覚えづらい単語もあるでしょうが，全単語に関してこれだけやれば，長文を読んでも知らない単語はほとんどなくなるでしょうし，英作文も自信を持って書けるようになります。

　けれども，そこでやめないでください。私たちの脳は，せっかく覚えたこともやがて忘れるようにできています。忘れないようするためには，あまり間をおかずに繰り返し確認するしかありません。ある有名大学を調査したところ，学生の卒業時の英語語彙は，入学時の半分ほどしかなかったそうです。これはあまりにもったいない。せっかく苦労して覚えた英単語は，なんとしても忘れないようにして頂きたい。心配しなくても，一度覚えたことなら，容易に再確認できるはずです。あきらめさえしなければ，英語は皆さんにとって一生便利なツールになってくれます。

　英語を学ぶことで，皆さんの世界が広がってゆくことを祈っています。

著者記す

『システム英単語 Basic〈5訂版対応〉フレーズ・単語書きこみワークブック』
本書の構成と使い方

★本書は『システム英単語 Basic〈5訂版〉』に準拠した，フレーズと単語の記憶を助けるための書きこみ式ワークブックです。章立てや単語番号などは単語帳に対応しています。

★第1章 Starting Stage ～第3章 Essential Stage は，フレーズ・単語が30個ずつ見開きで掲載されています（章末など，一部例外もあります）。見開き1列ごとにミニマル・フレーズ→エントリー単語の順に確認してもよいですし，左右ページごとにフレーズだけ／単語だけをまとめてチェックすることもできます。

★第4章 多義語の Brush Up はフレーズのみ，巻頭の基礎単語のチェックと巻末のジャンル別英単語は例文のみ，もしくは単語のみの掲載となっています。フレーズが複数ある多義語については，「2-1」「2-2」のように番号を振っています。

『システム英単語 Basic〈5訂版〉』の単語番号に対応しています。

本冊＝『システム英単語 Basic〈5訂版〉』での単語掲載ページです。

取り組んだ日付や，30個中いくつ覚えたかの記録等にも使えます。

フレーズと単語は見開き1列ごとに対応しています。

フレーズ書きこみ欄は，左右の英語／日本語フレーズを参考にして，英訳・和訳どちらの書きこみにも使えます。学習進度や目的に合わせた使い方をしてください。

単語は発音記号と意味を確認して，それぞれ3回ずつ書いて覚えましょう。左隣の欄を見ながら，単語→意味→単語と交互に訳す練習をしてもよいでしょう。

●：山折り
◆：谷折り　の目安です（p.5 参照）。
※多義語のページは対応していません。

単語の意味は，『システム英単語 Basic〈5訂版〉』で赤字になっている重要な意味を簡潔に載せてあります。try to V のように，頻出の熟語の形で掲載しているものもあります。

いろいろな使い方を工夫してみよう！

書きこんだ後も，
折りたたんで使えば
フレーズをまとめて
チェックするのに便利！

単語帳付属の赤シートや
下敷きなどを使って，重要ポイントを
くりかえしチェック！

黒字のフレーズ・単語も
別紙で隠してまるごと確認！
専用のノートを作っても◎

単語帳でくわしい意味・語法の
復習も忘れずに！
シリーズと一緒に使えば
記憶定着効果バツグン！

Contents

第4章　多義語の *Brush Up*

ジャンル別英単語

Key Sentences

週の曜日

暦の月

基礎単語のチェック

カタカナ英語のつづりと発音

不規則動詞の活用形

Introduction

"Well begun is half done." — *Aristotle*

* * *

始めよければ半ば成功。— アリストテレス

No.		Key Sentences	意　味
S-1	書き込み	"What is the purpose of your visit?" "Sightseeing."	「訪問の目的は何ですか?」 「観光です」
S-2	書き込み	"How long have you been in Hawaii?" "Hmm, let's see ... for over ten weeks."	「ハワイに来てどれくらいになりますか?」 「ふーむ, そうですね…10週間以上になります」
S-3	書き込み	"Have you ever been to Thailand?" "No, not yet."	「これまでにタイに行ったことはありますか?」 「いいえ, まだありません」
S-4	書き込み	I found a surprising fact about Brazil.	ブラジルについて驚くべき事実を見つけた。
S-5	書き込み	There is a factory several miles away from here.	ここから数マイル離れたところに工場がある。
S-6	書き込み	I have lived in the country since I *got* married.	私は結婚して以来その国に住んできた。
S-7	書き込み	Three months *have* pass*ed* *since* he went away.	彼がいなくなってから3ヵ月たつ。
S-8	書き込み	We gathered in front of the entrance of the hall.	私たちはホールの入口の正面に集まった。
S-9	書き込み	We crossed to the other side of the street.	私たちは道を渡って向こう側に行った。
S-10	書き込み	A group of five people went camping near a waterfall in the Philippines.	5人のグループがフィリピンの滝の近くへキャンプに行った。

No.		Key Sentences	意 味
S-11		"Excuse me. Can you tell me the way to the nearest bank?"	「すみません。一番近くの銀行へ行く道を教えていただけますか?」
		"Well, turn left at the second corner and you'll see it on your right."	「ええと、2つめの角を左に曲がりなさい。そうすると, 右側に見えます」
		"I see. Thanks."	「わかりました。ありがとう」
	書き込み		
S-12		"Excuse me. Is there a hotel around here?"	「すみません。このあたりにホテルはありますか?」
		"Yeah. Go straight along the street and turn left at the second traffic _light_."	「ええ。この道をまっすぐに行って2つめの信号を左に曲がりなさい」
	書き込み		
S-13		"How long does it take to get to the station?"	「駅に行くのにどれくらい時間がかかりますか?」
		"Sorry, I'm a stranger here myself."	「すみません, 私自身もこのあたりは不案内なんです」
		"Okay. Thank you anyway."	「わかりました。とにかくありがとう」
	書き込み		
S-14		I am afraid to travel by myself. I often get lost on my way to school.	私はこわくてひとりで旅行できない。学校に行く途中で迷うこともしばしばだ。
	書き込み		
S-15	書き込み	The castle is 800 meters above _sea_ level.	その城は海抜800メートルにある。
S-16	書き込み	He worked for a long time as a tour guide in California.	彼は長い間カリフォルニアで観光ガイドとして働いた。

No.	Key Sentences	意 味
S-17 □ 書き込み	I took a direct flight to Paris.	私はパリ直行便に乗った。
S-18 □ 書き込み	A kitten was approaching me.	子猫が私に近づいてきた。
S-19 □ 書き込み	He went down to the convenience store alone.	彼はひとりでコンビニへ行った。
S-20 □ 書き込み	"Would you help me?"	「手伝っていただけますか?」
	"Sure, what can I do for you?"	「はい, 何をしましょうか?」
S-21 □ 書き込み	Can I exchange this five-dollar bill *for* coins?	この5ドル札をコインに交換していただけますか?
S-22 □ 書き込み	Let's ask Greg for advice.	グレッグに助言を頼もう。
S-23 □ 書き込み	"I'm sure we'll have a good time together."	「一緒に楽しめると思うよ」
	"I think so, too."	「私もそう思う」
S-24 □ 書き込み	I'm looking forward to see*ing* you.	あなたに会えるのを楽しみにしています。
S-25 □ 書き込み	"*What's the* matter?"	「どうしたのですか?」
	"I have a headache and fever."	「頭痛がして, 熱があるのです」
	"That's too bad."	「それはかわいそうに」
S-26 □ 書き込み	"Hey, why don't you come with me?"	「やあ, 一緒に来ませんか?」
	"That's very kind of you."	「ご親切にありがとう」

No.	Key Sentences	意　味
	"Why don't we take a break?"	「休憩を取りませんか?」
	"Why not? Sounds _good_. By the way, what time is it?"	「うん, いいね。ところで, 今何時?」
	"It's about seven."	「7時くらいです」
S-27		
書き込み		
	"May I have your name?"	「お名前を教えていただけますか?」
	"Yes, my name is Norman Rockwell."	「はい, 私の名前はノーマン・ロックウェルです」
S-28		
書き込み		
	"Can I speak to Cathy?"	「キャシーと話せますか?」
	"Sorry, but she's out now. Would you like to leave a message?"	「すみませんが, 彼女は今外出しています。メッセージを残しますか?」
	"No, thank you. I'll call back later."	「いいえ, ありがとう。後でかけ直します」
S-29		
書き込み		
	"Will you introduce me to your friend?"	「あなたの友だちに私を紹介してくれませんか?」
	"Sure. This is Nao. She is an old friend from nursery school."	「ええ。こちらナオです。保育園からの古い友だちです」
S-30		
書き込み		
	"Here is my e-mail address."	「これが私の E メールアドレスです」
	"Thanks. I'll send you an e-mail by tomorrow."	「ありがとう。明日までに E メールを送ります」
S-31		
書き込み		

	単語	意味	書きこみ①	書きこみ②	書きこみ③
☐	**week** [wíːk] ウィーク	名 週 ◇wéekend　名 週末			
☐	**Sunday** [sʌ́ndei] サンデイ	名 日曜日　略 Sun. 源 Sun(太陽)+day(日)			
☐	**Monday** [mʌ́ndi] マンデイ	名 月曜日　略 Mon. 源 Mon(=moon／月)+day(日)			
☐	**Tuesday** [t(j)úːzdei] トゥーズデイ	名 火曜日 略 Tue.またはTues.			
☐	**Wednesday** [wénzdei] ウェンズデイ	名 水曜日　略 Wed.			
☐	**Thursday** [θə́ːrzdei] サーズデイ	名 木曜日 略 Thur.またはThurs.			
☐	**Friday** [fráidi] フライデイ	名 金曜日　略 Fri.			
☐	**Saturday** [sǽtərdei] サタデイ	名 土曜日　略 Sat.			

Introduction ★

No.	単語	意味	書きこみ①	書きこみ②	書きこみ③
☐	**January** [dʒǽnjuèri] ヂャニュエリ	名 1月　略 Jan.			
☐	**February** [fébjueri] フェビュエリ	名 2月　略 Feb.			
☐	**March** [mɑ́ːrtʃ] マーチ	名 3月　略 Mar.			
☐	**April** [éiprəl] エイプリル	名 4月　略 Ap. または Apr.			
☐	**May** [méi] メイ	名 5月			
☐	**June** [dʒúːn] ヂューン	名 6月　略 Jun.			
☐	**July** [dʒulái] ヂュライ	名 7月　略 Jul.			
☐	**August** [ɔ́ːgəst] オーガスト	名 8月　略 Aug.			
☐	**September** [septémbər] セプテンバ	名 9月　略 Sep. または Sept.			
☐	**October** [ɑktóubər] アクトウバ	名 10月　略 Oct.			
☐	**November** [nouvémbər] ノウヴェンバ	名 11月　略 Nov.			
☐	**December** [disémbər] ディセンバ	名 12月　略 Dec.			

No.	単語	意味	書きこみ①	書きこみ②	書きこみ③
1	**million** [míljən]	100万			
2	**travel** [trǽvl]	旅行			
3	**war** [wɔ́ːr]	戦争			
4	**attention** [əténʃən]	注意			
5	**motion** [móuʃən]	運動			
6	**front** [fránt]	前部			
7	**style** [stáil]	様式			
8	**voice** [vɔ́is]	声			
9	**position** [pəzíʃən]	位置			
10	**ship** [ʃíp]	船			
11	**symbol** [símbl]	象徴			
12	**god** [gád]	神			
13	**energy** [énərdʒi]	エネルギー			
14	**plane** [pléin]	飛行機			
15	**meat** [míːt]	肉			
16	**secret** [síːkrət]	秘密			
17	**childhood** [tʃáildhud]	子供時代			
18	**essay** [ései]	エッセイ			
19	**toy** [tɔ́i]	おもちゃ			
20	**gesture** [dʒéstʃər]	身ぶり			
21	**teenager** [tíːneidʒər]	10代の若者			
22	**umbrella** [ʌmbrélə]	傘			
23	**tail** [téil]	尾			
24	**wing** [wíŋ]	翼			
25	**rhythm** [ríðm]	リズム			
26	**pond** [pánd]	池			
27	**subway** [sʌ́bwei]	地下鉄			
28	**hobby** [hábi]	趣味			
29	**salad** [sǽləd]	サラダ			
30	**rock** [ráːk]	岩			

No.	単語	意味	書きこみ①	書きこみ②	書きこみ③
31	ghost [góust]	幽霊			
32	victory [víktəri]	勝利			
33	medicine [médəsn]	薬			
34	discount [dískaunt]	割引			
35	flag [flǽg]	旗			
36	glove [glʌ́v]	手ぶくろ			
37	problem [prábləm]	問題			
38	ocean [óuʃən]	海			
39	magazine [mǽgəzi:n]	雑誌			
40	button [bʌ́tn]	ボタン			
41	hole [hóul]	穴			
42	event [ivént]	できごと			
43	illness [ílnəs]	病気			
44	film [fílm]	映画			
45	earth [ə́:rθ]	地球			
46	blackboard [blǽkbɔ:rd]	黒板			
47	message [mésidʒ]	メッセージ			
48	wood [wúd]	木材			
49	typhoon [taifú:n]	台風			
50	smoke [smóuk]	煙			
51	business [bíznəs]	事業			
52	course [kɔ́:rs]	コース			
53	design [dizáin]	デザイン			
54	cafeteria [kæfətíəriə]	カフェテリア			
55	diary [dáiəri]	日記(帳)			
56	condition [kəndíʃən]	状態			
57	schedule [skédʒu:l]	計画			
58	frog [frág]	カエル			
59	train [tréin]	列車			
60	roof [rú:f]	屋根			

No.	単語	意味	書きこみ①	書きこみ②	書きこみ③
61	**return** [ritə́ːrn]	帰る			
62	**ride** [ráid]	乗る			
63	**burn** [bə́ːrn]	燃える			
64	**attack** [ətǽk]	～を攻撃する			
65	**hate** [héit]	～がいやだ			
66	**shoot** [ʃúːt]	～を撃つ			
67	**fall** [fɔ́ːl]	落ちる			
68	**drive** [dráiv]	運転する			
69	**fill** [fíl]	～を満たす			
70	**build** [bíld]	～を建設する			
71	**feel** [fíːl]	～を感じる			
72	**happen** [hǽpn]	起きる			
73	**carry** [kǽri]	～を運ぶ			
74	**popular** [pápjələr]	人気のある			
75	**safe** [séif]	安全な			
76	**quiet** [kwáiət]	静かな			
77	**weak** [wíːk]	弱い			
78	**hungry** [hʌ́ŋgri]	空腹な			
79	**wet** [wét]	ぬれた			
80	**grand** [grǽnd]	雄大な			
81	**double** [dʌ́bl]	2倍の			
82	**ill** [íl]	病気だ			
83	**dry** [drái]	乾燥した			
84	**full** [fúl]	いっぱいの			
85	**same** [séim]	同じ			
86	**modern** [mádərn]	現代の			
87	**sharp** [ʃáːrp]	鋭い			
88	**mild** [máild]	おだやかな			
89	**digital** [dídʒitl]	デジタルの			
90	**important** [impɔ́ːrtənt]	重要な			

★ Introduction

No.	単語	意味	書きこみ①	書きこみ②	書きこみ③
91	**wrong** [rɔ́(ː)ŋ]	悪い			
92	**normal** [nɔ́ːrml]	標準の			
93	**monthly** [mʌ́nθli]	月1回の			
94	**suddenly** [sʌ́dnli]	突然に			
95	**maybe** [méibi(ː)]	多分			
96	**forever** [fərévər]	永遠に			
97	**however** [hauévər]	しかし			
98	**below** [bilóu]	〜より下の方に			
99	**beside** [bisáid]	〜の横に			
100	**above** [əbʌ́v]	〜より上の方に			

	単語	意味	書きこみ①	書きこみ②	書きこみ③
☐	**accessory** [əksésəri]	アクセサリー			
☐	**album** [ǽlbəm]	アルバム			
☐	**alphabet** [ǽlfəbet]	アルファベット			
☐	**amateur** [ǽmətʃuər]	アマチュア			
☐	**box** [báks]	箱			
☐	**camera** [kǽmərə]	カメラ			
☐	**camp** [kǽmp]	キャンプ			
☐	**candle** [kǽndl]	ロウソク			
☐	**captain** [kǽptn]	キャプテン			
☐	**chorus** [kɔ́:rəs]	コーラス			
☐	**colorful** [kʌ́lərfl]	カラフルな			
☐	**computer** [kəmpjú:tər]	コンピュータ			
☐	**contest** [kántest]	コンテスト			
☐	**copy** [kápi]	コピー(する)			
☐	**corn** [kɔ́:rn]	コーン			
☐	**couple** [kʌ́pl]	カップル			
☐	**cute** [kjú:t]	かわいい			
☐	**cycling** [sáikliŋ]	サイクリング			
☐	**designer** [dizáinər]	デザイナー			
☐	**engine** [éndʒən]	エンジン			
☐	**fan** [fǽn]	(有名人などの)ファン			
☐	**fence** [féns]	フェンス			
☐	**gasoline** [gǽsəli:n]	ガソリン			
☐	**gold** [góuld]	金			
☐	**golden** [góuldn]	金の			
☐	**group** [grú:p]	グループ			
☐	**guitar** [gitá:r]	ギター			
☐	**gun** [gʌ́n]	銃			
☐	**handkerchief** [hǽŋkərtʃif]	ハンカチ			
☐	**heart** [há:rt]	心			

	単語	意味	書きこみ①	書きこみ②	書きこみ③
☐	**hotel** [houtél]	ホテル			
☐	**idea** [aidíːə]	考え			
☐	**jogging** [dʒágiŋ]	ジョギング			
☐	**juice** [dʒúːs]	ジュース			
☐	**kick** [kík]	キック			
☐	**league** [líːg]	リーグ			
☐	**lemon** [lémən]	レモン			
☐	**lucky** [lʌ́ki]	ラッキー			
☐	**machine** [məʃíːn]	機械			
☐	**magic** [mǽdʒik]	マジック			
☐	**manager** [mǽnidʒər]	経営者			
☐	**marathon** [mǽrəθɑn]	マラソン			
☐	**medal** [médl]	メダル			
☐	**menu** [ménjuː]	メニュー			
☐	**metal** [metl]	金属			
☐	**mirror** [mírər]	鏡			
☐	**monster** [mánstər]	怪物			
☐	**musician** [mjuːzíʃən]	音楽家			
☐	**nonsense** [nánsens]	ナンセンス			
☐	**omelet** [áməlɑt]	オムレツ			
☐	**panel** [pǽnl]	パネル			
☐	**passport** [pǽspɔːrt]	パスポート			
☐	**pattern** [pǽtərn]	パターン			
☐	**percentage** [pərséntidʒ]	百分率			
☐	**photograph** [fóutəgræf]	写真			
☐	**pocket** [pákət]	ポケット			
☐	**police** [pəlíːs]	警察			
☐	**pot** [pát]	ポット			
☐	**prince** [príns]	王子			
☐	**princess** [prínsəs]	王女			

	単語	意味	書きこみ①	書きこみ②	書きこみ③
☐	**queen** [kwíːn]	女王			
☐	**record** 名 [rékərd] 動 [rikɔ́ːd]	記録（する）			
☐	**report** [ripɔ́ːrt]	報告（する）			
☐	**rival** [ráivl]	ライバル			
☐	**rocket** [rákət]	ロケット			
☐	**rope** [róup]	ロープ			
☐	**silver** [sílvər]	銀			
☐	**sofa** [sóufə]	ソファ			
☐	**spaghetti** [spəgéti]	スパゲッティ			
☐	**staff** [stǽf]	スタッフ			
☐	**stamp** [stǽmp]	スタンプ			
☐	**title** [táitl]	タイトル			
☐	**towel** [táuəl]	タオル			
☐	**wedding** [wédiŋ]	結婚式			

原形 意味	過去形	過去分詞	書きこみ 原形	書きこみ 過去形	書きこみ 過去分詞
□ **bring** 持ってくる	brought	brought			
□ **build** 建てる	built	built			
□ **buy** 買う	bought	bought			
□ **catch** つかまえる	caught	caught			
□ **cut** 切る	cut	cut			
□ **dig** 掘る	dug	dug			
□ **feel** 感じる	felt	felt			
□ **find** 見つける	found	found			
□ **hang** つるす	hung	hung			
□ **have** 持っている	had	had			
□ **hear** 聞く	heard	heard			
□ **hit** たたく,打つ	hit	hit			
□ **hold** 持つ,抱く	held	held			
□ **hurt** 傷つける	hurt	hurt			
□ **keep** 保つ	kept	kept			
□ **lay** 置く	laid	laid			
□ **leave** 出発する	left	left			
□ **lose** なくす	lost	lost			
□ **make** 作る	made	made			
□ **mean** 意味する	meant	meant			
□ **meet** 会う	met	met			
□ **put** 置く	put	put			
□ **read** 読む	read	read			
□ **say** 言う	said	said			
□ **sell** 売る	sold	sold			
□ **send** 送る	sent	sent			
□ **shine** 輝く	shone / shined	shone / shined			

Introduction

	原形 意味	過去形	過去分詞	書きこみ 原形	書きこみ 過去形	書きこみ 過去分詞
☐	**sit** 座る	sat	sat			
☐	**sleep** 眠る	slept	slept			
☐	**spend** 費やす	spent	spent			
☐	**stand** 立つ	stood	stood			
☐	**teach** 教える	taught	taught			
☐	**tell** 言う	told	told			
☐	**think** 思う	thought	thought			
☐	**understand** 理解する	understood	understood			
☐	**win** 勝つ	won	won			

原形 意味	過去形	過去分詞	書きこみ 原形	書きこみ 過去形	書きこみ 過去分詞
☐ **be** 〜である	was・were	been			
☐ **become** 〜になる	became	become			
☐ **begin** 始める	began	begun			
☐ **bite** 噛む	bit	bitten			
☐ **blow** 吹く	blew	blown			
☐ **break** 壊す	broke	broken			
☐ **choose** 選ぶ	chose	chosen			
☐ **come** 来る	came	come			
☐ **do** する	did	done			
☐ **draw** 描く	drew	drawn			
☐ **drink** 飲む	drank	drunk			
☐ **drive** 運転する	drove	driven			
☐ **eat** 食べる	ate	eaten			
☐ **fall** 落ちる	fell	fallen			
☐ **fly** 飛ぶ	flew	flown			
☐ **forget** 忘れる	forgot	forgot／forgotten			
☐ **get** 得る	got	got／gotten			
☐ **give** 与える	gave	given			
☐ **go** 行く	went	gone			
☐ **grow** 成長する	grew	grown			
☐ **hide** 隠す	hid	hidden			
☐ **know** 知っている	knew	known			
☐ **lie** 横になる	lay	lain			
☐ **ride** 乗る	rode	ridden			
☐ **ring** 鳴る	rang／rung	rung			
☐ **rise** のぼる	rose	risen			
☐ **run** 走る	ran	run			

Introduction ★

25

	原形 意味	過去形	過去分詞	書きこみ 原形	書きこみ 過去形	書きこみ 過去分詞
☐	**see** 見る	saw	seen			
☐	**shake** 振る	shook	shaken			
☐	**show** 見せる	showed	shown / showed			
☐	**sing** 歌う	sang	sung			
☐	**speak** 話す	spoke	spoken			
☐	**steal** 盗む	stole	stolen			
☐	**swim** 泳ぐ	swam	swum			
☐	**take** 取る	took	taken			
☐	**throw** 投げる	threw	thrown			
☐	**wear** 着ている	wore	worn			
☐	**write** 書く	wrote	written			

Stage 1

Starting Stage

"A word is enough to a wise man."

＊　＊　＊

賢者にはひとことで十分。（一を聞いて十を知る）

No.	英語フレーズ	フレーズ書きこみ	日本語フレーズ
1	help him find a room		彼が部屋を見つけるのを手伝う
2	try *to* find a word		言葉を見つけようとする
3	hold flowers in both hands		両手で花を持つ
4	grow *up* in the country		田舎で育つ
5	Let me talk to her.		彼女と話をさせてください
6	He seems *to be* happy.		彼は幸せそうだ
7	enjoy read*ing* comics		マンガを読むのを楽しむ
8	create new problems		新しい問題を生み出す
9	choose the best answer		もっともよい答えを選ぶ
10	spend time think*ing*		考えるのに時間を費やす
11	He appears *to be* sleeping.		彼は眠っているように見える
12	lie in bed		ベッドで横になる
13	lie to her father		彼女の父にうそをつく
14	arrive *at* the station		駅に着く
15	discover a new world		新しい世界を発見する
16	act as a group		集団として行動する
17	The sun rises in the east.		東に太陽が昇る
18	Don't forget *to* call him.		彼に電話するのを忘れないで
19	hang a picture on the wall		壁に絵をかける
20	I wish I could fly.		飛べればいいのにと思う
21	*be* born with a talent for music		音楽の才能を持って生まれる
22	win a prize		賞を勝ち取る
23	fight *against* disease		病気と戦う
24	pick *up* a coin		コインを拾い上げる
25	She *is* dressed *in* black.		彼女は黒を着ている
26	communicate *with* each other		お互いに考えを伝え合う
27	The number of children dropped.		子供の数が減った
28	throw a pie at him		彼にパイを投げる
29	promise *to* go with him		彼と行くと約束する
30	separate gold *from* sand		砂から金を分離する

単語	意味	書きこみ①	書きこみ②	書きこみ③	No.
help [hélp]	〜を助ける				1
try to V [trái]	Vしようとする				2
hold [hóuld]	〜を保持する				3
grow [gróu]	育つ				4
let A ＋原形V [lét]	AにVさせてやる				5
seem (to be) A [síːm]	Aのように思える				6
enjoy [indʒɔ́i]	〜を楽しむ				7
create [kriéit]	〜を生み出す				8
choose [tʃúːz]	(〜を)選ぶ				9
spend [spénd]	〜を費やす				10
appear [əpíər]	〜のように見える				11
lie¹ [lái]	横になる				12
lie² [lái]	うそをつく				13
arrive [əráiv]	着く				14
discover [diskʌ́vər]	〜を発見する				15
act [ǽkt]	行動する				16
rise [ráiz]	上がる				17
forget [fərgét]	〜を忘れる				18
hang [hǽŋ]	〜をかける				19
wish (that) 〜 [wíʃ]	〜であればいいのにと思う				20
born [bɔ́ːrn]	生まれる				21
win [wín]	〜に勝つ				22
fight (against) A [fáit]	Aと戦う				23
pick A up [pík]	Aを拾い上げる				24
dress [drés]	服を着る				25
communicate [kəmjúːnəkeit]	考えを伝える				26
drop [drάp]	落ちる				27
throw [θróu]	〜を投げる				28
promise [prάməs]	(〜を)約束する				29
separate [sépəreit] 形 [sépərət]	〜を分ける				30

1
Starting

No.	英語フレーズ	フレーズ書きこみ	日本語フレーズ
31 ☐	**pull** the rope hard		ロープを強く引く
32 ☐	**push** a button		ボタンを押す
33 ☐	**hunt** wild animals		野生の動物を狩る
34 ☐	**hide** the truth *from* them		彼らに真実を隠す
35 ☐	**lay** a hand on the shoulder		肩に手を置く
36 ☐	**join** the baseball club		野球部に入る
37 ☐	**climb** Mount Everest		エベレストに登る
38 ☐	**relax** on the sofa		ソファでくつろぐ
39 ☐	**invite** her *to* dinner		彼女をディナーに招待する
40 ☐	**ring** a bell		ベルを鳴らす
41 ☐	**collect** information		情報を集める
42 ☐	**gather** food		食料を集める
43 ☐	**wake** up early		早く目が覚める
44 ☐	Stress *is* **linked** *to* illness.		ストレスは病気と関係がある
45 ☐	**repeat** what he just said		彼が言ったことを繰り返す
46 ☐	**mix** yellow *with* blue		青と黄色を混ぜる
47 ☐	**recycle** paper		紙を再生利用する
48 ☐	**roll** down the street		道を転がる
49 ☐	I **requested** that she *send* me money.		彼女にお金を送ってくれと頼んだ
50 ☐	**lift** a heavy rock		重い岩を持ち上げる
51 ☐	The wind is **blowing** from the north.		北から風が吹いている
52 ☐	**dislike** washing dishes		皿洗いが嫌いだ
53 ☐	**sail** west from Spain		スペインから西に船旅をする
54 ☐	**limit** the speed		速度を制限する
55 ☐	**comment** *on* the news		そのニュースについて論評する
56 ☐	**introduce** you *to* my friend		友人に君を紹介する
57 ☐	a **barking** dog		ほえる犬
58 ☐	**dig** a hole in the ground		地面に穴を掘る
59 ☐	**wrap** a birthday present		誕生日の贈り物を包む
60 ☐	The sun is **shining**.		太陽が輝いている

単語	意味	書きこみ①	書きこみ②	書きこみ③	No.
pull [púl]	〜を引く				31
push [púʃ]	〜を押す				32
hunt [hʌ́nt]	(〜を)狩る				33
hide [háid]	〜を隠す				34
lay [léi]	〜を置く				35
join [dʒɔ́in]	〜に参加する				36
climb [kláim]	〜に登る				37
relax [rilǽks]	リラックスする				38
invite [inváit]	〜を招待する				39
ring [ríŋ]	鳴る				40
collect [kəlékt]	〜を集める				41
gather [gǽðər]	〜を集める				42
wake [wéik]	目を覚ます				43
be linked to A [líŋkt]	Aと関係がある				44
repeat [ripíːt]	(〜を)繰り返して言う				45
mix [míks]	〜を混ぜる				46
recycle [risáikl]	〜を再生利用する				47
roll [róul]	〜を巻く				48
request [rikwést]	〜を頼む				49
lift [líft]	〜を持ち上げる				50
blow [blóu]	吹く				51
dislike [disláik]	〜が嫌いだ				52
sail [séil]	航行する				53
limit [límit]	〜を制限する				54
comment [kάment]	論評する				55
introduce [intrədʤúːs]	〜を紹介する				56
bark [bάːrk]	ほえる				57
dig [díg]	〜を掘る				58
wrap [rǽp]	〜を包む				59
shine [ʃáin]	輝く				60

1

Starting

No.	英語フレーズ	フレーズ書きこみ	日本語フレーズ
61	shut the door		ドアを閉める
62	enter the room		部屋に入る
63	knock *on* the door		ドアをノックする
64	lend him 5,000 yen		彼に5,000円を貸す
65	mark the beginning of a new age		新時代の幕開けを示す
66	pass through the gate		門を通る
67	shout *at* him		彼にどなる
68	Imagine there's no hunger.		飢えがなくなると想像しなさい
69	I hope someday you'll join us.		君がいつか参加することを望む
70	He's planning *to* visit India.		彼はインドを訪問するつもりである
71	plant trees		木を植える
72	record data		データを記録する
73	She reported that he was alive.		彼が生きていると彼女は報告した
74	We were shocked to hear the news.		私たちはその知らせを聞いてショックを受けた
75	steal money *from* a bank		銀行からお金を盗む
76	Barking dogs seldom bite.		ほえる犬はめったにかまない
77	It began to rain.		雨が降りはじめた
78	I disagree *with* you *on* this point.		この点で私はあなたと意見が異なる
79	boil water		湯をわかす
80	fried chicken		フライドチキン
81	stay *in* this place		この場所にとどまる
82	get a new job		新しい仕事につく
83	the fact *that* the earth is round		地球が丸いという事実
84	stop at a red light		赤信号で止まる
85	people from different cultures		異文化の人々
86	*in* the 21st century		21世紀に
87	people of all ages		あらゆる年齢の人々
88	get information about a product		製品に関する情報を得る
89	the cost of living		生活費
90	buy new land		新しい土地を買う

単語	意味	書きこみ①	書きこみ②	書きこみ③	No.
shut [ʃʌ́t]	～を閉じる				61
enter [éntər]	～に入る				62
knock [nák]	ノックする				63
lend [lénd]	～を貸す				64
mark [máːrk]	～に印を付ける				65
pass [pǽs]	(～を)通る				66
shout [ʃáut]	叫ぶ				67
imagine [imǽdʒin]	～と想像する				68
hope (that) SV [hóup]	SVを望む				69
plan [plǽn]	(～を)計画する				70
plant [plǽnt]	～を植える				71
record [rikɔ́ːrd] 名 [rékərd]	～を記録する				72
report [ripɔ́ːrt]	～を報告する				73
shock [ʃák]	～にショックを与える				74
steal [stíːl]	～を盗む				75
bite [báit]	(～を)かむ				76
begin [biɡín]	はじまる				77
disagree [disəɡríː]	意見が異なる				78
boil [bɔ́il]	～をゆでる				79
fry [frái]	～を油であげる				80
place [pléis]	場所				81
job [dʒáb]	仕事				82
fact [fǽkt]	事実				83
light [láit]	光				84
culture [kʌ́ltʃər]	文化				85
century [séntʃəri]	世紀				86
age [éidʒ]	年齢				87
information [infərméiʃən]	情報				88
living [líviŋ]	生きること				89
land [lǽnd]	土地				90

1
Starting

No.	英語フレーズ	フレーズ書きこみ	日本語フレーズ
91	the history of science		科学の歴史
92	people *in the* past		過去の人々
93	make plans for *the* future		将来の計画をたてる
94	He is in good health.		彼は健康状態がいい
95	an open space		空いている場所
96	*on* the other side of the road		道の反対側
97	It is against the law to drive drunk.		飲酒運転は法律違反だ
98	her dream *of* being a singer		彼女の歌手になりたいという夢
99	a graduation ceremony		卒業式
100	*at* that moment		その瞬間に
101	pay a high price		高い値段を支払う
102	the Amazon rain forest		アマゾンの雨林
103	How is *the* weather?		天気はどうですか
104	*have* conversations with Americans		アメリカ人と会話する
105	the fear *of* making mistakes		まちがうのではないかという不安
106	the ability *to* think		考える能力
107	*have* a car accident		自動車事故にあう
108	*the* international community		国際社会
109	higher than average		平均より高い
110	his success *in* business		彼のビジネスでの成功
111	animals and human beings		動物と人間
112	*in* my opinion		私の意見では
113	have a good memory		記憶力がよい
114	put in *a* bit *of* sugar		少し砂糖を入れる
115	come into contact *with* Europeans		ヨーロッパ人と接触する
116	high blood pressure		高血圧
117	the belief *that* people can change		人は変わりうるという信念
118	There is no doubt *that* he is alive.		彼が生きていることに疑いはない
119	the date of the meeting		その会議の日程
120	modern technology		現代の科学技術

単語	意味	書きこみ①	書きこみ②	書きこみ③	No.
history [hístəri]	歴史				91
past [pǽst]	過去				92
future [fjúːtʃər]	未来				93
health [hélθ]	健康				94
space [spéis]	空間				95
side [sáid]	側				96
law [lɔ́ː]	法律				97
dream [dríːm]	夢				98
ceremony [sérəmouni]	儀式				99
moment [móumənt]	瞬間				100
price [práis]	値段				101
forest [fɔ́(ː)rəst]	森林				102
weather [wéðər]	天気				103
conversation [kɑnvərséiʃən]	会話				104
fear [fíər]	恐れ				105
ability [əbíləti]	能力				106
accident [ǽksədənt]	事故				107
community [kəmjúːnəti]	社会				108
average [ǽvəridʒ]	平均				109
success [səksés]	成功				110
human being [hjúːmən bíːiŋ]	人間				111
opinion [əpínjən]	意見				112
memory [méməri]	記憶				113
bit [bít]	少量				114
contact [kɑ́ntækt]	接触				115
blood [blʌ́d]	血				116
belief [bilíːf]	信念				117
doubt [dáut]	疑い				118
date [déit]	日付				119
technology [teknálədʒi]	科学技術				120

1 Starting

No.	英語フレーズ	フレーズ書きこみ	日本語フレーズ
121	have three meals a day		1日に3回食事をとる
122	the sale of books		本の販売
123	Cycling is a lot of fun.		サイクリングはとても楽しい
124	an American tourist		アメリカ人の観光客
125	the main goal of this study		この研究の主たる目的
126	None of us know him.		私たちは誰も彼を知らない
127	make a big noise		大きな音を立てる
128	a direct flight to New York		ニューヨークへの直行便
129	send a letter *by* air mail		航空郵便で手紙を送る
130	run out of gas		ガソリンがなくなる
131	*do* great damage *to* the human body		人体に大きな害を与える
132	the answer sheet		解答用紙
133	work on a farm		農場で働く
134	test a new drug on animals		動物で新薬をテストする
135	a post on the website		ウェブサイトの投稿
136	the smell of popcorn		ポップコーンのにおい
137	a nurse in a nursing home		介護施設の看護師
138	We have a special guest today.		今日は特別なお客がある
139	work as a tour guide in Paris		パリで観光ガイドとして働く
140	the flow of water		水の流れ
141	be *in a* hurry to catch a train		電車に乗ろうと急いでいる
142	a large-scale market		大規模な市場
143	have a job interview		就職の面接を受ける
144	tell a joke		冗談を言う
145	*a* series *of* events		一連の出来事
146	make an error *in* grammar		文法の誤りを犯す
147	answer *on* the spot		その場で答える
148	Fill in the blanks.		空欄を埋めなさい
149	become a movie actor		映画俳優になる
150	study mathematics		数学を学ぶ

単語	意味	書きこみ①	書きこみ②	書きこみ③	No.
meal [míːl]	食事				121
sale [séil]	販売				122
fun [fʌ́n]	楽しみ				123
tourist [túərist]	観光客				124
goal [góul]	目的				125
none [nʌ́n]	どれも…ない				126
noise [nɔ́iz]	音				127
flight [fláit]	飛行				128
mail [méil]	郵便				129
gas [gǽs]	ガス				130
damage [dǽmidʒ]	害				131
sheet [ʃíːt]	１枚の紙				132
farm [fɑ́ːrm]	農場				133
drug [drʌ́g]	薬				134
post [póust]	郵便				135
smell [smél]	におい				136
nurse [nə́ːrs]	看護師				137
guest [gést]	客				138
guide [gáid]	案内（係）				139
flow [flóu]	流れ				140
hurry [hə́ːri]	急ぎ				141
scale [skéil]	規模				142
interview [íntərvjuː]	面接				143
joke [dʒóuk]	冗談				144
a series of A [síəri(ː)z]	一連の A				145
error [érər]	誤り				146
spot [spɑ́t]	地点				147
blank [blǽŋk]	空欄				148
actor [ǽktər]	俳優				149
mathematics [mæθəmǽtiks]	数学				150

No.	英語フレーズ	フレーズ書きこみ	日本語フレーズ
151	Help me with my homework.		宿題を手伝って
152	*take* a bath every day		毎日風呂に入る
153	walk two blocks		2ブロック歩く
154	US soldiers in Iraq		イラクのアメリカ兵士
155	make a long journey		長い旅行をする
156	the host country		主催国
157	the shortest route *to* Korea		韓国への最短経路
158	eat from plates of gold		金の皿から食べる
159	have *a sense of* humor		ユーモアのセンスがある
160	sit on the green grass		緑の草の上に座る
161	pay $1,000 *in* cash		1,000ドルを現金で払う
162	the west coast of Australia		オーストラリアの西海岸
163	get a *high* salary		高い給料をもらう
164	become a national hero		国民的英雄になる
165	the gap *between* rich and poor		貧富の格差
166	be caught by a guard		守衛につかまる
167	pass the test *with* ease		楽に試験に受かる
168	join the British army		イギリス陸軍に入る
169	the Battle of Sekigahara		関ヶ原の戦い
170	teach pupils		生徒に教える
171	in the second paragraph		第2段落に
172	the mystery of life		生命の謎
173	coal, oil, and gas		石炭, 石油, ガス
174	ride a bike		自転車に乗る
175	*make a* fool *of* him		彼をばかにする
176	*for the* sake *of* children		子供たちのために
177	He's a nice guy.		彼はいい男だ
178	*get* a driver's license		運転免許を取る
179	*in* a hopeless situation		希望のない状況で
180	put a label on a bottle		ビンにラベルを貼る

単語	意味	書きこみ①	書きこみ②	書きこみ③	No.
homework [hóumwə:rk]	宿題				151
bath [bǽθ]	入浴				152
block [blák]	ブロック				153
soldier [sóuldʒər]	兵士				154
journey [dʒə́:rni]	旅行				155
host [hóust]	主催者				156
route [rú:t]	道				157
plate [pléit]	皿				158
humor [hjú:mər]	ユーモア				159
grass [grǽs]	草				160
cash [kǽʃ]	現金				161
coast [kóust]	海岸地域				162
salary [sǽləri]	給料				163
hero [hí:rou]	英雄				164
gap [gǽp]	格差				165
guard [gá:rd]	守衛				166
ease [í:z]	楽				167
army [á:rmi]	軍隊				168
battle [bǽtl]	戦い				169
pupil [pjú:pl]	生徒				170
paragraph [pǽrəgræf]	段落				171
mystery [místəri]	謎				172
coal [kóul]	石炭				173
bike [báik]	自転車				174
fool [fú:l]	ばか				175
sake [séik]	ため				176
guy [gái]	男				177
license [láisəns]	免許				178
situation [sitʃuéiʃən]	状況				179
label [léibl]	ラベル				180

1
Starting

No.	英語フレーズ	フレーズ書きこみ	日本語フレーズ
181	give aid *to* poor countries		貧しい国に援助を与える
182	Change your clothes.		服を着替えなさい
183	the long shadow of a man		男の長い影
184	put the meat in the refrigerator		肉を冷蔵庫に入れる
185	*at* the bottom of the sea		海の底で
186	a $100,000 bank loan		10万ドルの銀行ローン
187	put my hands on my knees		ひざに手を置く
188	20 square miles		20平方マイル
189	go down the stairs		階段を下りる
190	*have* a bad headache		ひどい頭痛がする
191	*in* their cultural setting		彼らの文化的環境で
192	go into a cave		洞くつに入る
193	the root of many misunderstandings		多くの誤解の根源
194	cry out with joy		喜びで叫び声をあげる
195	walk on the shore		海岸を歩く
196	go to bed *at* midnight		夜の12時に寝る
197	a poet and a novelist		詩人と小説家
198	a report in a scientific journal		科学雑誌の報告
199	receive the Nobel Prize		ノーベル賞を受ける
200	a tool for learning		学習の道具
201	talk about the topic		その話題について話す
202	a sound wave		音波
203	in many areas of the world		世界の多くの地域で
204	have control *over* the market		市場を支配する
205	live *in* harmony *with* nature		自然と調和して暮らす
206	a balance *between* work and play		仕事と遊びのバランス
207	heat energy from the sun		太陽からの熱エネルギー
208	*have* a wonderful experience		すばらしい経験をする
209	a *police* officer		警察官
210	a traffic accident		交通事故

単語	意味	書きこみ①	書きこみ②	書きこみ③	No.
aid [éid]	援助				181
clothes [klóuz]	衣服				182
shadow [ʃǽdou]	影				183
refrigerator [rifrídʒəreitər]	冷蔵庫				184
bottom [bátəm]	底				185
loan [lóun]	ローン				186
knee [níː]	ひざ				187
square [skwéər]	正方形				188
stairs [stéərz]	階段				189
headache [hédeik]	頭痛				190
setting [sétiŋ]	背景				191
cave [keiv]	洞くつ				192
root [rúːt]	根				193
joy [dʒɔ́i]	喜び				194
shore [ʃɔ́ːr]	岸				195
midnight [mídnait]	夜の12時				196
poet [póuət]	詩人				197
journal [dʒɔ́ːrnl]	雑誌				198
prize [práiz]	賞				199
tool [túːl]	道具				200
topic [tápik]	話題				201
wave [wéiv]	波				202
area [éəriə]	地域				203
control [kəntróul]	支配				204
harmony [háːrməni]	調和				205
balance [bǽləns]	バランス				206
heat [híːt]	熱				207
experience [ikspíəriəns]	経験				208
officer [ɔ́fəsər]	役人				209
traffic [trǽfik]	交通（量）				210

Starting

No.	英語フレーズ	フレーズ書きこみ	日本語フレーズ
211	Love your neighbor as yourself.		自分を愛するように隣人を愛せ
212	I am in the seventh grade.		私は7年生 (=中1) です
213	Anybody can do that.		誰でもそれはできる
214	I can't see anything.		何も見えない
215	a *flight* attendant		客室乗務員
216	the tiger in the cage		おりの中のトラ
217	talk on the cell phone		携帯電話でしゃべる
218	eat the fish with chopsticks		はしで魚を食べる
219	customers of the restaurant		そのレストランの客
220	look up the word in the dictionary		辞書で単語を引く
221	a computer engineer		コンピュータ技術者
222	get lost in the fog		霧の中で迷う
223	fight for freedom		自由を求めて戦う
224	send a package to France		フランスに小包を送る
225	husband and wife		夫と妻
226	a kindergarten teacher		幼稚園の先生
227	*Good* luck!		幸運を祈ります!
228	a Greek temple		ギリシャの神殿
229	the movement of her eyes		彼女の目の動き
230	*a* piece *of* paper		紙1枚
231	go sightseeing in Venice		ヴェニスに観光に行く
232	*have* trouble find*ing* a job		仕事を見つけるのに苦労する
233	He is different *from* other people.		彼は他の人と違う
234	I'm sure that he'll pass.		彼は合格すると私は確信している
235	This book is difficult to understand.		この本を理解するのは難しい
236	have *at* least three children		少なくとも3人の子供を持つ
237	global warming		地球の温暖化
238	several years ago		数年前に
239	learn a foreign language		外国語を学ぶ
240	my whole life		私の全人生

単語	意味	書きこみ①	書きこみ②	書きこみ③	No.
neighbor [néibər]	近所の人				211
grade [gréid]	学年				212
anybody [énibɑdi]	誰でも				213
anything [éniθiŋ]	何でも				214
attendant [əténdənt]	接客係				215
cage [kéidʒ]	おり				216
cell phone [sél fóun]	携帯電話				217
chopstick [tʃɑ́pstik]	はし				218
customer [kʌ́stəmər]	客				219
dictionary [díkʃəneri]	辞書				220
engineer [endʒəníər]	技術者				221
fog [fɔ́(ː)g]	霧				222
freedom [fríːdəm]	自由				223
package [pǽkidʒ]	包装				224
husband [hʌ́zbənd]	夫				225
kindergarten [kíndərgɑːrtn]	幼稚園				226
luck [lʌ́k]	運				227
temple [templ]	寺院				228
movement [múːvmənt]	運動				229
piece [píːs]	ひとつ				230
sightseeing [sáitsiːiŋ]	観光				231
trouble [trʌ́bl]	悩み				232
different [dífərənt]	異なる				233
be sure of A [ʃúər]	Aを確信している				234
difficult [dífikʌlt]	難しい				235
least [líːst]	最も小さい				236
global [glóubəl]	世界的な				237
several [sévərəl]	いくつかの				238
foreign [fɔ́ːrən]	外国の				239
whole [hóul]	すべての				240

No.	英語フレーズ	フレーズ書きこみ	日本語フレーズ
241	Leave me alone.		私をひとりにしておいて
242	It is necessary to stop him.		彼を止めることが必要だ
243	the main reason		主な理由
244	Germany is famous *for* its beer.		ドイツはビールで有名だ
245	be afraid *of* making mistakes		誤りを犯すことを恐れる
246	All people are created equal.		全ての人は平等につくられている
247	fall into a deep sleep		深い眠りに落ちる
248	be busy *with* part-time work		バイトでいそがしい
249	The same *is* true *of* the Japanese.		同じ事が日本人にも当てはまる
250	carry a heavy bag		重いかばんを運ぶ
251	It is dangerous to swim in the river.		その川で泳ぐのは危険だ
252	a wide street		幅の広い道路
253	a very exciting game		すごくおもしろいゲーム
254	It's impossible to understand him.		彼を理解するのは不可能だ
255	our daily lives		私たちの日常生活
256	He was surprised *to* hear it.		彼はそれを聞いて驚いた
257	No Smoking in Public Places		公共の場では禁煙
258	a tired body		疲れた体
259	get angry *with* him		彼に腹を立てる
260	wild animals		野生動物
261	a dark-haired girl		黒い髪の少女
262	find a dead body		死体を発見する
263	Be careful not to make this mistake.		この誤りをしないよう気をつけなさい
264	ordinary people		普通の人々
265	stay at a cheap hotel		安いホテルに泊まる
266	Central America		中央アメリカ
267	She is friendly to others.		彼女は人に親切だ
268	Language is unique *to* humans.		言語は人間特有のものだ
269	I'm glad *to* hear that.		それを聞いてうれしい
270	find another way		もう1つの道を見つける

単語	意味	書きこみ①	書きこみ②	書きこみ③	No.
alone [əlóun]	ひとりで				241
necessary [nésəseri]	必要な				242
main [méin]	主な				243
famous [féiməs]	有名な				244
afraid [əfréid]	恐れる				245
equal [íːkwəl]	平等な				246
deep [díːp]	深い				247
busy [bízi]	いそがしい				248
true [trúː]	真実の				249
heavy [hévi]	重い				250
dangerous [déindʒərəs]	危険な				251
wide [wáid]	広い				252
exciting [iksáitiŋ]	わくわくさせる				253
impossible [impásəbl]	不可能な				254
daily [déili]	日常の				255
surprised [sərpráizd]	驚いている				256
public [pʌ́blik]	公の				257
tired [táiərd]	疲れた				258
angry [ǽŋgri]	腹を立てた				259
wild [wáild]	野生の				260
dark [dáːrk]	黒い				261
dead [déd]	死んだ				262
careful [kéərfl]	気をつける				263
ordinary [ɔ́ːrdəneri]	普通の				264
cheap [tʃíːp]	安い				265
central [séntrəl]	中央の				266
friendly [fréndli]	親切な				267
unique [juːníːk]	独特の				268
glad [glǽd]	うれしい				269
another [ənʌ́ðər]	もう1つの				270

1 Starting

No.	英語フレーズ	フレーズ書きこみ	日本語フレーズ
271	in the bright light		明るい光の中で
272	regular working hours		通常の勤務時間
273	poor countries		貧しい国々
274	keep a constant speed		一定の速度を保つ
275	for commercial use		商業用に
276	a local television station		地方のテレビ局
277	It is fair to say so.		そう言うのは正当だ
278	Be honest with yourself.		自分に正直になりなさい
279	He *is* proud *of* himself.		彼は自分に誇りを持っている
280	*fall* asleep in class		授業中に眠りこむ
281	make a loud noise		騒々しい音を立てる
282	the chief reason for his success		彼が成功した主な理由
283	overseas travel		海外旅行
284	a very clever monkey		とても利口なサル
285	upper-class people		上流階級の人々
286	wash dirty dishes		汚れた皿を洗う
287	a smart shopper		賢い買い物客
288	the royal family		王室
289	*be* crazy *about* fishing		釣りに夢中だ
290	*be* absent *from* school		学校を欠席している
291	speak in a gentle voice		やさしい声で話す
292	delicious Indian food		おいしいインド料理
293	walk on thin ice		薄い氷の上を歩く
294	elegant design		優雅なデザイン
295	smooth plastic		すべすべしたプラスチック
296	feel lonely without you		あなたがいなくてさびしい
297	It is clear that he knows the answer.		彼が答えを知っているのは明らかだ
298	have a personal interest		個人的な興味を持つ
299	my lovely daughter		私のかわいい娘
300	books for the blind		目の不自由な人のための本

単語	意味	書きこみ①	書きこみ②	書きこみ③	No.
bright [bráit]	明るい				271
regular [régjələr]	いつもの				272
poor [púər]	貧しい				273
constant [kánstənt]	不変の				274
commercial [kəmə́ːrʃl]	商業の				275
local [lóukəl]	その土地の				276
fair [féər]	正当な				277
honest [ánəst]	正直な				278
proud [práud]	誇りを持っている				279
asleep [əslíːp]	眠って				280
loud [láud]	大きい				281
chief [tʃíːf]	主な				282
overseas [óuvərsíːz]	海外の				283
clever [klévər]	利口な				284
upper [ʌ́pər]	上の方の				285
dirty [də́ːrti]	汚れた				286
smart [smáːrt]	利口な				287
royal [rɔ́iəl]	国王の				288
crazy [kréizi]	狂っている				289
absent [ǽbsənt]	いない				290
gentle [dʒéntl]	やさしい				291
delicious [dilíʃəs]	おいしい				292
thin [θín]	薄い				293
elegant [éligənt]	優雅な				294
smooth [smúːð]	なめらかな				295
lonely [lóunli]	孤独な				296
clear [klíər]	明らかな				297
personal [pə́ːrsənl]	個人の				298
lovely [lʌ́vli]	美しい				299
blind [bláind]	盲目の				300

1
Starting

No.	英語フレーズ	フレーズ書きこみ	日本語フレーズ
301	play an active part		積極的な役割を演じる
302	search for intelligent life in space		宇宙の知的生命体を捜す
303	a round table		丸いテーブル
304	a broad street		幅の広い通り
305	from the outside world		外の世界から
306	He looks happy, but actually he is sad.		彼はうれしそうだが実は悲しいのだ
307	watch TV rather *than* study		勉強するよりテレビを見る
308	drink coffee almost every day		ほとんど毎日コーヒーを飲む
309	be quite different		まったく異なっている
310	She hasn't arrived yet.		彼女はまだ到着していない
311	Perhaps it's true.		ひょっとするとそれは本当かもしれない
312	The river is beautiful, especially in summer.		その川は特に夏美しい
313	I like it simply because it's useful.		それが好きなのは単に役立つからだ
314	use robots instead *of* people		人の代わりにロボットを使う
315	Either you *or* he is lying.		君か彼のどちらかがうそをついている
316	He finally found a job.		彼はやっと仕事を見つけた
317	It is strange indeed.		それは実に奇妙だ
318	Ask someone else.		だれか他の人に聞いて
319	Neither Tom *nor* his wife is happy.		トムも奥さんも幸せではない
320	move forward		前へ進む
321	a highly developed society		高度に発達した社会
322	go abroad		外国に行く
323	go straight to the room		まっすぐ部屋に行く
324	look straight ahead		まっすぐ前を見る
325	live apart *from* my parents		親から離れて暮らす
326	"Did you win?" "Naturally."		「勝ったのか?」「当然さ」
327	Unfortunately, he didn't come.		残念ながら彼は来なかった
328	speak Japanese fairly well		日本語をかなり上手に話す
329	His image was badly damaged.		彼のイメージはひどく傷ついた
330	move back and forth		前後に動く

単語	意味	書きこみ①	書きこみ②	書きこみ③	No.
active [ǽktiv]	活動的な				301
intelligent [intélidʒənt]	知的な				302
round [ráund]	丸い				303
broad [brɔ́ːd]	幅の広い				304
outside [autsáid]	外の				305
actually [ǽktʃuəli]	実は				306
A rather than B [rǽðər]	BよりもむしろA				307
almost [ɔ́ːlmoust]	ほとんど				308
quite [kwáit]	まったく				309
yet [jét]	まだ				310
perhaps [pərhǽps]	ことによると				311
especially [ispéʃəli]	特に				312
simply [símpli]	単に				313
instead [instéd]	代わりに				314
either A or B [íːðər]	AかBのどちらか				315
finally [fáinəli]	やっと				316
indeed [indíːd]	実に				317
else [éls]	他の				318
neither A nor B [níːðər]	AもBも(…し)ない				319
forward [fɔ́ːrwərd]	前へ				320
highly [háili]	高度に				321
abroad [əbrɔ́ːd]	外国へ				322
straight [stréit]	まっすぐ				323
ahead [əhéd]	前へ				324
apart [əpáːrt]	離れて				325
naturally [nǽtʃərəli]	当然				326
unfortunately [ʌnfɔ́ːrtʃənətli]	あいにく				327
fairly [féərli]	かなり				328
badly [bǽdli]	ひどく				329
forth [fɔ́ːrθ]	前へ				330

1 Starting

No.	英語フレーズ	フレーズ書きこみ	日本語フレーズ
331	go downtown		中心街へ行く
332	He came back three years later.		彼は3年後に戻ってきた
333	go upstairs to the bedroom		2階の寝室に行く
334	I've already seen the movie.		その映画はすでに見た
335	live far *from* home		家から遠く離れて暮らす
336	Thank you anyway.		とにかくありがとう
337	You can call me anytime.		いつでも私に電話していいよ
338	You can go anywhere.		どこでも行っていいよ
339	Bill also met Tracy.		ビルもトレーシーに会った
340	*turn* left at the corner		かどを左に曲がる
341	both the husband *and* wife		夫も妻も両方
342	Have you ever been to Italy?		今までにイタリアに行ったことがありますか
343	everywhere in the world		世界のいたるところで
344	halfway *through* the movie		その映画の中ほどで
345	It's moving toward him.		それは彼の方に向かって動いている
346	live without a car		車なしで暮らす
347	during the war		戦争の間
348	Would you stay here while I'm away?		私が留守の間ここにいてくれますか
349	Though it was late, I called him.		遅かったけれども彼に電話をした
350	Although it was raining, I went out.		雨だったが私は外出した

単語	意味	書きこみ①	書きこみ②	書きこみ③	No.
downtown [dáuntáun]	町の中心へ				331
later [léitər]	後で				332
upstairs [ʌpstéərz]	階上へ				333
already [ɔːlrédi]	すでに				334
far [fáːr]	遠くに				335
anyway [éniwei]	とにかく				336
anytime [énitaim]	いつでも				337
anywhere [énihweər]	どこでも				338
also [ɔ́ːlsou]	〜もまた				339
left [léft]	左へ				340
both [bóuθ]	両方とも				341
ever [évər]	今までに				342
everywhere [évrihweər]	いたるところで				343
halfway [hǽfwéi]	中ほどで				344
toward [tɔ́ːrd]	前〜の方に				345
without [wiðáut]	前〜なしで				346
during [djúəriŋ]	前〜の間ずっと				347
while [hwáil]	接〜している間に				348
though [ðóu]	接〜けれども				349
although [ɔːlðóu]	接〜けれども				350

Stage 2

"In the beginning was the Word" — *John*

* * *

はじめに言葉ありき。— ヨハネによる福音書

No.	英語フレーズ	フレーズ書きこみ	日本語フレーズ
351	follow her advice		彼女の助言に従う
352	consider the problem seriously		真剣にその問題を考える
353	increase *by* 20%		20%増加する
354	expect you *to* arrive soon		君がすぐ着くことを予期する
355	decide *to* tell the truth		真実を語る決意をする
356	develop a unique ability		特異な能力を発達させる
357	provide him *with* information		彼に情報を与える
358	continue *to* grow fast		急速に成長し続ける
359	The list includes his name.		リストは彼の名前を含んでいる
360	remain silent		黙ったままでいる
361	reach the mountain top		山頂に達する
362	allow him *to* go out		彼に外出を許可する
363	*be* forced *to* work		働くよう強制される
364	offer help *to* the poor		貧しい人に援助を申し出る
365	realize the error		まちがいを悟る
366	suggest a new way		新しいやり方を提案する
367	require more attention		もっと注意を必要とする
368	worry *about* money		お金のことを心配する
369	wonder where he has gone		彼はどこに行ったのかと思う
370	The car cost me $50,000.		その車には5万ドルかかった
371	tend *to* get angry		腹を立てがちである
372	Everything depends *on* him.		すべては彼しだいだ
373	share a room *with* a friend		友人と部屋を共有する
374	demand more freedom		もっと自由を要求する
375	support the president		大統領を支持する
376	hire many young people		多くの若者を雇う
377	regard him *as* a friend		彼を友達とみなす
378	This story *is* based *on* fact.		この話は事実に基づいている
379	improve living conditions		生活状態を向上させる
380	recognize the importance		重要性を認める

単語	意味	書きこみ①	書きこみ②	書きこみ③	No.
follow [fálou]	〜に続く				351
consider [kənsídər]	〜を考慮する				352
increase [inkrí:s] 名 [ínkri:s]	増える				353
expect [ikspékt]	〜を予期する				354
decide [disáid]	〜することを決意する				355
develop [divéləp]	発達する				356
provide [prəváid]	〜を供給する				357
continue [kəntínju:]	続く				358
include [inklú:d]	〜を含む				359
remain [riméin]	ままでいる				360
reach [rí:tʃ]	〜に着く				361
allow [əláu]	〜を許可する				362
force [fɔ́:rs]	〜を強制する				363
offer [áfər]	〜を申し出る				364
realize [ríəlaiz]	〜を悟る				365
suggest [sʌdʒést]	〜と提案する				366
require [rikwáiər]	〜を必要とする				367
worry [wə́:ri]	心配する				368
wonder [wʌ́ndər]	〜かと疑問に思う				369
cost [kɔ́(:)st]	〜を要する				370
tend to V [ténd]	Vする傾向がある				371
depend on A [dipénd]	Aに依存する				372
share [ʃéər]	〜を分け合う				373
demand [dimǽnd]	〜を要求する				374
support [səpɔ́:rt]	〜を支持する				375
hire [háiər]	〜を雇う				376
regard A as B [rigá:rd]	AをBだと思う				377
A be based on B [béist]	AがBに基づいている				378
improve [imprú:v]	〜を向上させる				379
recognize [rékəgnaiz]	〜を認める				380

2
Fundamental

No.	英語フレーズ	フレーズ書きこみ	日本語フレーズ
381	notice the color change		色彩の変化に気づく
382	You *are* supposed *to* wear a seat belt.		シートベルトを締めることになっている
383	raise both hands		両手を上げる
384	prefer tea *to* coffee		コーヒーよりお茶を好む
385	cheer *up* the patients		患者たちを元気づける
386	suffer heavy damage		ひどい損害を受ける
387	describe the lost bag		なくしたバッグの特徴を言う
388	prevent him *from* sleeping		彼が眠るのをさまたげる
389	reduce energy costs		エネルギー費を減らす
390	mistake salt *for* sugar		塩を砂糖とまちがえる
391	prepare a room *for* a guest		客のために部屋を準備する
392	encourage children *to* read		子供に読書をすすめる
393	prove *to be* true		本当だとわかる
394	treat him like a child		子供みたいに彼をあつかう
395	establish a company		会社を設立する
396	stress-related illness		ストレスと関係のある病気
397	compare Japan *with* China		日本と中国を比較する
398	spread the tablecloth		テーブルクロスを広げる
399	What does this word refer *to*?		この語は何を指示するか
400	supply the city *with* water		その都市に水を供給する
401	gain useful knowledge		有益な知識を得る
402	destroy forests		森林を破壊する
403	apply the rule *to* every case		全ての場合に規則を当てはめる
404	seek help from the police		警察に助けを求める
405	search *for* the stolen car		盗難車を捜す
406	He claims that he saw a UFO.		彼はUFOを見たと主張する
407	draw a map		地図を描く
408	refuse *to* give up hope		希望を捨てるのを拒む
409	respond *to* questions		質問に答える
410	Never mention it again.		二度とそのことを口にするな

単語	意味	書きこみ①	書きこみ②	書きこみ③	No.
notice [nóutis]	〜に気づく				381
suppose [səpóuz]	〜だと思う				382
raise [réiz]	〜を上げる				383
prefer [prifə́:r]	〜をより好む				384
cheer [tʃíər]	〜を励ます				385
suffer [sʌ́fər]	〜を経験する				386
describe [diskráib]	〜を描写する				387
prevent [privént]	〜をさまたげる				388
reduce [ridjú:s]	〜を減らす				389
mistake [mistéik]	〜を誤解する				390
prepare [pripéər]	準備をする				391
encourage [inkə́:ridʒ]	はげます				392
prove [prú:v]	〜だとわかる				393
treat [trí:t]	〜をあつかう				394
establish [estǽbliʃ]	〜を設立する				395
relate [riléit]	関係がある				396
compare [kəmpéər]	〜を比較する				397
spread [spréd]	〜を広げる				398
refer to A [rifə́:r]	Aを指示する				399
supply [səplái]	〜を供給する				400
gain [géin]	〜を得る				401
destroy [distrɔ́i]	〜を破壊する				402
apply [əplái]	当てはまる				403
seek [síːk]	〜を求める				404
search for A [sə́:rtʃ]	Aを捜す				405
claim [kléim]	〜と主張する				406
draw [drɔ́:]	〜を引っぱる				407
refuse [rifjú:z]	〜を断る				408
respond to A [rispánd]	Aに返答する				409
mention [ménʃən]	〜について述べる				410

2 Fundamental

No.	英語フレーズ	フレーズ書きこみ	日本語フレーズ
411	judge a person *by* his looks		人を外見で判断する
412	The plane is approaching Chicago.		飛行機はシカゴに接近している
413	I admit *that* I was wrong.		自分がまちがっていたと認める
414	reflect the mood of the times		時代の気分を反映する
415	perform the job		仕事を遂行する
416	a very boring movie		すごく退屈な映画
417	survive in the jungle		ジャングルで生き残る
418	Words represent ideas.		言葉は考えを表す
419	argue *that* he is right		彼は正しいと主張する
420	*take* freedom *for* granted		自由を当然と考える
421	The data indicate *that* he is right.		データは彼が正しいことを示す
422	The book belongs *to* Howard.		その本はハワードのものだ
423	acquire a language		言語を習得する
424	reply *to* his letter		彼の手紙に返事をする
425	feed a large family		大勢の家族を養う
426	escape *from* reality		現実から逃避する
427	replace the old system		古い制度に取って代わる
428	reveal a surprising fact		驚くべき事実を明らかにする
429	Japan *is* surrounded by the sea.		日本は海に囲まれている
430	The job suits you.		その仕事は君に合っている
431	the estimated population of Japan		日本の推定人口
432	aim *at* the Asian market		アジア市場をねらう
433	earn money for the family		家族のためにお金をかせぐ
434	My memory began to decline.		記憶力が低下し始めた
435	*can't* afford *to* buy a Ford		フォードの車を買う余裕がない
436	be confused by her anger		彼女の怒りに当惑する
437	graduate *from* high school		高校を卒業する
438	vary from country to country		国によって変わる
439	remove the cover		カバーを取り除く
440	insist *on* going to France		フランスに行くと言い張る

単語	意味	書きこみ①	書きこみ②	書きこみ③	No.
judge [dʒʌ́dʒ]	〜を判断する				411
approach [əpróutʃ]	（〜に）接近する				412
admit [ədmít]	〜を認める				413
reflect [riflékt]	〜を反映する				414
perform [pərfɔ́ːrm]	〜を行う				415
bore [bɔ́ːr]	〜をうんざりさせる				416
survive [sərváiv]	生き残る				417
represent [reprizént]	〜を表す				418
argue [áːrgjuː]	〜と主張する				419
grant [grǽnt]	〜を認める				420
indicate [índikeit]	〜を指し示す				421
belong [bilɔ́(ː)ŋ]	所属している				422
acquire [əkwáiər]	〜を習得する				423
reply [riplái]	返事をする				424
feed [fíːd]	〜にエサをやる				425
escape [iskéip]	逃げる				426
replace [ripléis]	〜に取って代わる				427
reveal [rivíːl]	〜を明らかにする				428
surround [səráund]	〜を取り囲む				429
suit [súːt]	〜に合う				430
estimate [éstəmeit] 名 [éstəmət]	〜を推定する				431
aim at A [éim]	Aをねらう				432
earn [ɔ́ːrn]	〜をもうける				433
decline [dikláin]	衰退する				434
afford [əfɔ́ːrd]	〜をする余裕がある				435
confuse [kənfjúːz]	〜を当惑させる				436
graduate from A [grǽdʒueit] 名 [grǽdʒuət]	Aを卒業する				437
vary [véəri]	変わる				438
remove [rimúːv]	〜を移す				439
insist [insíst]	〜と主張する				440

2 Fundamental

No.	英語フレーズ	フレーズ書きこみ	日本語フレーズ
441	examine every record		あらゆる記録を調べる
442	remind him *of* the promise		彼に約束を思い出させる
443	contribute *to* world peace		世界平和に貢献する
444	warn him *of* the danger		彼に危険を警告する
445	connect the computer *to* the Internet		コンピュータをインターネットにつなぐ
446	match him in power		力で彼に匹敵する
447	focus *on* the problem		その問題に焦点を合わせる
448	reject the proposal		提案を拒否する
449	convince him *that* it is true		それは本当だと彼に確信させる
450	Health is associated *with* happiness.		健康は幸福と関連している
451	rush into the hospital		病院へ急いで行く
452	stress the need for information		情報の必要性を強調する
453	attract his attention		彼の注意を引きつける
454	rely *on* their power		彼らの力に頼る
455	regret leaving home		家を出たのを後悔する
456	adopt a new system		新しいシステムを採用する
457	shake the bottle well		ビンをよく振る
458	hurt her feelings		彼女の気持ちを傷つける
459	operate a computer with a mouse		マウスでコンピュータを操作する
460	Exercise extends life.		運動は寿命を延ばす
461	blame others *for* the failure		失敗を他人のせいにする
462	The book consists *of* six lessons.		その本は6課で構成されている
463	persuade them *to* go back		彼らを説得して帰らせる
464	admire her work		彼女の仕事に感嘆する
465	be disappointed *with* the test results		試験の結果に失望する
466	expand business overseas		海外へ事業を拡大する
467	preserve forests		森林を保護する
468	struggle *to* get free		自由になろうともがく
469	arrange the meeting		会議の手はずを整える
470	disturb his sleep		彼の睡眠をさまたげる

単語	意味	書きこみ①	書きこみ②	書きこみ③	No.
examine [ɪgzǽmɪn]	〜を調査する				441 ☐
remind A of B [rɪmáɪnd]	AにBのことを思い出させる				442 ☐
contribute to A [kəntríbjuːt]	Aに貢献する				443 ☐
warn [wɔ́ːrn]	〜に警告する				444 ☐
connect [kənékt]	〜をつなぐ				445 ☐
match [mǽtʃ]	〜に匹敵する				446 ☐
focus [fóukəs]	焦点を合わせる				447 ☐
reject [rɪdʒékt]	〜を断る				448 ☐
convince [kənvíns]	〜を納得させる				449 ☐
associate A with B [əsóuʃieɪt]	AをBに関連づける				450 ☐
rush [rʌ́ʃ]	急いで行く				451 ☐
stress [strés]	〜を強調する				452 ☐
attract [ətrǽkt]	〜を引きつける				453 ☐
rely on A [rɪláɪ]	Aに頼る				454 ☐
regret [rɪgrét]	〜を後悔する				455 ☐
adopt [ədápt]	〜を採用する				456 ☐
shake [ʃéɪk]	〜を振る				457 ☐
hurt [hə́ːrt]	〜を傷つける				458 ☐
operate [ápəreɪt]	作動する				459 ☐
extend [ɪksténd]	〜を広げる				460 ☐
blame [bléɪm]	〜を非難する				461 ☐
consist of A [kənsíst]	Aで構成されている				462 ☐
persuade [pərswéɪd]	〜を説得する				463 ☐
admire [ədmáɪər]	〜に感心する				464 ☐
disappoint [dɪsəpɔ́ɪnt]	〜を失望させる				465 ☐
expand [ɪkspǽnd]	（〜を）拡大する				466 ☐
preserve [prɪzə́ːrv]	〜を保護する				467 ☐
struggle [strʌ́gl]	苦闘する				468 ☐
arrange [əréɪndʒ]	〜の手はずを整える				469 ☐
disturb [dɪstə́ːrb]	〜をさまたげる				470 ☐

2

Fundamental

No.	英語フレーズ	フレーズ書きこみ	日本語フレーズ
471	employ foreign workers		外国人労働者を雇う
472	engage *in* volunteer activities		ボランティア活動に従事する
473	an abandoned pet		捨てられたペット
474	display prices		価格を示す
475	encounter many difficulties		数々の困難に出会う
476	amuse students with jokes		冗談で学生を笑わせる
477	Sorry to bother you, but ...		おじゃましてすみませんが…
478	concentrate *on* what he is saying		彼の話に集中する
479	adapt *to* a new culture		新しい文化に適応する
480	be puzzled by the problem		その問題に頭を悩ませる
481	appeal *to* his feelings		彼の感情に訴えかける
482	combine song and dance		歌と踊りを組み合わせる
483	delay his arrival		彼の到着を遅らせる
484	repair the car		車を修理する
485	a fascinating story		夢中にさせる物語
486	Pardon me.		ごめんなさい
487	import food from abroad		海外から食料を輸入する
488	remark that he is kind		彼は親切だと述べる
489	reserve a room at a hotel		ホテルの部屋を予約する
490	at an amazing speed		驚異的な速さで
491	frightening experiences		ぞっとするような経験
492	release him *from* work		仕事から彼を解放する
493	rent an apartment		アパートを借りる
494	recover *from* illness		病気から回復する
495	I suspect that he is a spy.		私は彼がスパイではないかと思う
496	deliver a message *to* a friend		友人に伝言を渡す
497	identify people by their eyes		目で人の本人確認をする
498	The office *is* located *in* the area.		オフィスはその地域にある
499	a car manufacturing company		車を製造する会社
500	occupy a high position		高い地位を占める

単語	意味	書きこみ①	書きこみ②	書きこみ③	No.
employ [emplɔ́i]	～を雇う				471
engage in A [engéidʒ]	Aに従事する				472
abandon [əbǽndən]	～を捨てる				473
display [displéi]	～を展示する				474
encounter [inkáuntər]	～に偶然出会う				475
amuse [əmjúːz]	～を楽しませる				476
bother [báðər]	～に面倒をかける				477
concentrate [kánsəntreit]	集中する				478
adapt [ədǽpt]	～を適応させる				479
puzzle [pʌ́zl]	～を当惑させる				480
appeal to A [əpíːl]	Aに訴える				481
combine [kəmbáin]	～を結合させる				482
delay [diléi]	～を遅らせる				483
repair [ripéər]	～を修理する				484
fascinate [fǽsəneit]	～を夢中にさせる				485
pardon [páːrdn]	～を許す				486
import [impɔ́ːrt] 名 [ímpɔːrt]	～を輸入する				487
remark [rimáːrk]	（～と）述べる				488
reserve [rizɔ́ːrv]	～を予約する				489
amaze [əméiz]	～を驚嘆させる				490
frighten [fráitn]	～をおびえさせる				491
release [rilíːs]	～を解放する				492
rent [rent]	～を賃借りする				493
recover from A [rikʌ́vər]	Aから回復する				494
suspect [səspékt] 名 [sʌ́spekt]	～ではないかと思う				495
deliver [dilívər]	～を配達する				496
identify [aidéntəfai]	～の正体をつきとめる				497
be located in A [lóukeitid]	Aに位置する				498
manufacture [mænjəfǽktʃər]	～を製造する				499
occupy [ákjəpai]	～を占める				500

2
Fundamental

No.	英語フレーズ	フレーズ書きこみ	日本語フレーズ
501	own a house		家を所有している
502	be exposed *to* danger		危険にさらされる
503	translate a novel *into* English		小説を英語に翻訳する
504	cure him *of* his illness		彼の病気を治す
505	perceive danger		危険に気づく
506	adjust *to* a new school		新しい学校に慣れる
507	be alarmed by the noise		その音にぎょっとする
508	assist him in his work		彼の仕事を手伝う
509	a frozen stream		凍った小川
510	spoil the party		パーティを台無しにする
511	shift gears		ギアを変える
512	be embarrassed by the mistake		そのまちがいが恥ずかしい
513	approve *of* their marriage		2人の結婚を承認する
514	weigh 65 kilograms		65キロの重さがある
515	stretch my legs		足を広げる
516	participate *in* the meeting		会議に参加する
517	exhibit Picasso's works		ピカソの作品を展示する
518	I owe my success *to* you.		私の成功はあなたのおかげだ
519	celebrate his birthday		彼の誕生日を祝う
520	trees decorated *with* lights		電球で飾られた木々
521	forgive him *for* being late		彼の遅刻を許す
522	*be* seated on the bench		ベンチで座っている
523	*be* injured in the accident		その事故で負傷する
524	sew a wedding dress		ウエディングドレスを縫う
525	the result of the test		テストの結果
526	features of human language		人類の言語の特徴
527	the problems of modern society		現代社会の問題
528	a water wheel		水車
529	put a high value on education		教育に高い価値をおく
530	the greenhouse effect of CO_2		二酸化炭素の温室効果

単語	意味	書きこみ①	書きこみ②	書きこみ③	No.
own [óun]	〜を所有している				501
expose A to B [ikspóuz]	AをBにさらす				502
translate [trǽnsleit]	〜を翻訳する				503
cure [kjúər]	〜を治療する				504
perceive [pərsí:v]	〜を知覚する				505
adjust [ədʒʌ́st]	慣れる				506
alarm [əlá:rm]	〜をぎょっとさせる				507
assist [əsíst]	（〜を）助ける				508
freeze [frí:z]	凍りつく				509
spoil [spɔ́il]	〜を台無しにする				510
shift [ʃíft]	〜を変える				511
embarrass [imbǽrəs]	〜を困惑させる				512
approve [əprú:v]	賛成する				513
weigh [wéi]	〜の重さがある				514
stretch [strétʃ]	〜を広げる				515
participate in A [pɑ:rtísipeit]	Aに参加する				516
exhibit [igzíbit]	〜を展示する				517
owe A to B [óu]	AはBのおかげだ				518
celebrate [séləbreit]	〜を祝う				519
decorate [dékəreit]	〜を装飾する				520
forgive [fərgív]	〜を許す				521
be seated [sí:tid]	座っている				522
injure [índʒər]	〜を傷つける				523
sew [sóu]	〜を縫う				524
result [rizʌ́lt]	結果				525
feature [fí:tʃər]	特徴				526
society [səsáiəti]	社会				527
wheel [hwí:l]	車輪				528
value [vǽlju:]	価値				529
effect [ifékt]	効果				530

2 Fundamental

No.	英語フレーズ	フレーズ書きこみ	日本語フレーズ
531	individuals in society		社会の中の個人
532	*have* a bad influence *on* children		子供に悪い影響を与える
533	charge a fee for the service		サービス料を請求する
534	*at* the rate of 40% a year		年40%の割合で
535	a sign of spring		春のきざし
536	water and gas service		水道とガスの事業
537	advances *in* technology		科学技術の進歩
538	Laughter is the best medicine.		笑いは最高の良薬だ
539	produce new materials		新しい物質を作る
540	a center of heavy industry		重工業の中心地
541	an attempt *to* break the record		記録を破ろうとする試み
542	US trade with France		アメリカとフランスの貿易
543	You've *made* progress *in* English.		君の英語は進歩した
544	*make* an excuse to leave early		早く帰るための言い訳をする
545	the custom of tipping		チップを払う習慣
546	Read the following passage.		次の一節を読みなさい
547	the market economy		市場経済
548	the tracks of a lion		ライオンの足跡
549	use public transportation		公共交通機関を使う
550	a government official		政府の役人
551	love at first sight		一目ぼれ
552	a taste of lemon		レモンの味
553	a wide range of information		広範囲の情報
554	make an appointment *with* the doctor		医者に予約する
555	a doctor and a patient		医者と患者
556	a business project		事業計画
557	Would you *do* me a favor?		頼みをきいてもらえませんか
558	differ in appearance		外見が違う
559	*run the* risk of losing money		お金を失う危険を冒す
560	costs and benefits of the business		仕事のコストと利益

単語	意味	書きこみ①	書きこみ②	書きこみ③	No.
individual [ìndəvídʒuəl]	個人				531
influence [ínfluəns]	影響				532
fee [fíː]	謝礼				533
rate [réit]	割合				534
sign [sáin]	印				535
service [sə́ːrvəs]	（公益）事業				536
advance [ədvǽns]	前進				537
laughter [lǽftər]	笑い				538
material [mətíəriəl]	物質				539
industry [índəstri]	工業				540
attempt [ətémpt]	試み				541
trade [tréid]	貿易				542
progress [prágres] 動 [prəgrés]	進歩				543
excuse [ikskjúːs] 動 [ikskjúːz]	言い訳				544
custom [kʌ́stəm]	習慣				545
passage [pǽsidʒ]	一節				546
economy [ikánəmi]	経済				547
track [trǽk]	小道				548
transportation [trænspərtéiʃən]	交通機関				549
official [əfíʃəl]	役人				550
sight [sáit]	見ること				551
taste [téist]	味				552
range [réindʒ]	範囲				553
appointment [əpɔ́intmənt]	約束				554
patient [péiʃənt]	患者				555
project [prádʒekt] 動 [prədʒékt]	計画				556
favor [féivər]	好意				557
appearance [əpíərəns]	外見				558
risk [rísk]	危険				559
benefit [bénəfit]	利益				560

2 Fundamental

No.	英語フレーズ	フレーズ書きこみ	日本語フレーズ
561	residents of New York		ニューヨークの住民
562	their relatives and friends		彼らの親戚と友達
563	a mountain region		山岳地方
564	unique characteristics		ユニークな特徴
565	feel a sharp pain		鋭い痛みを感じる
566	a pair of *identical* twins		一組の一卵性双生児
567	*on* special occasions		特別な場合に
568	the principle of free trade		自由貿易の原則
569	the history department		歴史学科
570	It is my duty to help you.		君を助けるのが私の義務だ
571	the scene of the accident		事故の現場
572	avoid *traffic* jams		交通渋滞を避ける
573	the spirit of fair play		フェアプレーの精神
574	the medium of communication		コミュニケーションの手段
575	mass production		大量生産
576	gather a large audience		大勢の観客を集める
577	the most important element		最も重要な要素
578	global climate change		地球規模の気候変動
579	the French Revolution		フランス革命
580	the first quarter of this century		今世紀の最初の4分の1
581	a room with little furniture		家具の少ない部屋
582	the human brain		人間の脳
583	CO_2 in the earth's atmosphere		地球の大気中の二酸化炭素
584	private property		私有財産
585	a reward *for* hard work		努力の報酬
586	national security		国家の安全保障
587	give a cry of delight		喜びの声をあげる
588	a deserted road in the desert		砂漠の人影のない道
589	people from different backgrounds		経歴の違う人々
590	a trend *toward* fewer children		少子化の傾向

単語	意味	書きこみ①	書きこみ②	書きこみ③	No.
resident [rézidənt]	住民				561
relative [rélətiv]	親族				562
region [ríːdʒən]	地域				563
characteristic [kærəktərístik]	特徴				564
pain [péin]	苦痛				565
twin [twín]	双子の一方				566
occasion [əkéiʒən]	場合				567
principle [prínsəpl]	原理				568
department [dipáːrtmənt]	部門				569
duty [djúːti]	義務				570
scene [síːn]	場面				571
jam [dʒǽm]	渋滞				572
spirit [spírət]	精神				573
medium [míːdiəm]	手段				574
mass [mǽs]	一般大衆				575
audience [ɔ́ːdiəns]	聴衆				576
element [éləmənt]	要素				577
climate [kláimit]	気候				578
revolution [revəljúːʃən]	革命				579
quarter [kwɔ́ːrtər]	4分の1				580
furniture [fə́ːrnitʃər]	家具				581
brain [bréin]	脳				582
atmosphere [ǽtməsfiər]	大気				583
property [prápərti]	財産				584
reward [riwɔ́ːrd]	報酬				585
security [sikjúərəti]	安全				586
delight [diláit]	大喜び				587
desert [dézərt] 動 [dizə́ːrt]	砂漠				588
background [bǽkɡraund]	背景				589
trend [trénd]	傾向				590

2 Fundamental

No.	英語フレーズ	フレーズ書きこみ	日本語フレーズ
591	get 20% of the vote		20%の票を得る
592	a negative impact *on* the environment		環境に対する悪い影響
593	educational institutions		教育機関
594	social interaction *with* others		他人との社会的交流
595	an alternative *to* oil		石油の代わりになるもの
596	*do* no harm *to* children		子供に害を与えない
597	a travel agency		旅行代理店
598	people's great capacity *to* learn		人間のすばらしい学習能力
599	the Italian minister		イタリアの大臣
600	a hospital volunteer		病院で働くボランティア
601	*have* access *to* the Internet		インターネットを利用できる
602	large quantities *of* data		ぼう大な量のデータ
603	a branch *of* science		科学の一分野
604	a common language		共通の言語
605	a rough sketch		大ざっぱなスケッチ
606	He *is* likely *to* win.		彼が勝つ可能性が高い
607	serious social problems		深刻な社会問題
608	a particular character		特有の性質
609	information available *to* everyone		みんなが利用できる情報
610	bilingual children		二言語使用の子どもたち
611	I *am* ready *to* start.		出発の用意ができている
612	the correct answer		正しい答え
613	be familiar *with* Japanese culture		日本の文化にくわしい
614	physical beauty		肉体美
615	The book is worth read*ing*.		その本は読む価値がある
616	be involved *in* the accident		事故に巻き込まれている
617	I had a fantastic time.		私はすばらしい時をすごした
618	her private life		彼女の私生活
619	an obvious mistake		明白なまちがい
620	a native language		母語

単語	意味	書きこみ①	書きこみ②	書きこみ③	No.
vote [vóut]	投票				591
impact [ímpækt]	影響				592
institution [instətʃúːʃən]	機関				593
interaction [intərǽkʃən]	交流				594
alternative [ɔːltə́ːrnətiv]	代わりのもの				595
harm [háːrm]	害				596
agency [éidʒənsi]	機関				597
capacity [kəpǽsəti]	能力				598
minister [mínəstər]	大臣				599
volunteer [vɑləntíər]	ボランティア				600
access [ǽkses] [æksés]	利用する権利				601
quantity [kwántəti]	量				602
branch [brǽntʃ]	枝				603
common [kámən]	共通の				604
rough [rʌ́f]	荒い				605
likely [láikli]	ありそうな				606
serious [síəriəs]	深刻な				607
particular [pərtíkjulər]	ある特定の				608
available [əvéiləbl]	手に入る				609
bilingual [bailíŋgwl]	二言語使用の				610
ready [rédi]	用意ができた				611
correct [kərékt]	正しい				612
familiar [fəmíljər]	よく知られた				613
physical [fízikəl]	身体の				614
be worth A [wə́ːrθ]	Aの価値がある				615
be involved in A [inválvd]	Aに関係している				616
fantastic [fæntǽstik]	すばらしい				617
private [práivit]	個人の				618
obvious [ábviəs]	明白な				619
native [néitiv]	母国の				620

No.	英語フレーズ	フレーズ書きこみ	日本語フレーズ
621	a complex system		複雑なシステム
622	I'*m* willing *to* pay for good food.		おいしいものにお金を払ってもかまわない
623	the current international situation		今日の国際状況
624	male workers		男性の労働者
625	the proper use of words		言葉の適切な使い方
626	He is capable *of* doing the job.		彼はその仕事をする能力がある
627	He is independent *of* his parents.		彼は親から独立している
628	positive thinking		積極的な考え方
629	a pleasant experience		楽しい経験
630	a significant difference		重要な違い
631	the former president		前大統領
632	a chemical reaction		化学反応
633	be upset by the accident		事故で動揺している
634	from the previous year		前の年から
635	keep calm		冷静でいる
636	a specific individual		特定の個人
637	health-conscious Americans		健康を意識するアメリカ人
638	be superior *to* others		他の人よりすぐれている
639	an efficient use of energy		効率のよいエネルギーの使い方
640	fundamental human rights		基本的人権
641	a narrow street		狭い通り
642	a reasonable explanation		理にかなった説明
643	feel nervous about the future		将来のことで不安になる
644	The brothers look alike.		その兄弟は似ている
645	domestic violence		家庭内暴力
646	a negative answer		否定的な答え
647	make a moral judgment		道徳的な判断をする
648	be eager *to* study in the US		アメリカ留学を熱望する
649	the brain's remarkable ability		脳のすばらしい能力
650	drive away evil spirits		悪い霊を追い払う

単語	意味	書きこみ①	書きこみ②	書きこみ③	No.
complex [kəmpléks] 名 [kámpleks]	複雑な				621
be willing to V [wíliŋ]	Vする気がある				622
current [kə́:rənt]	最新の				623
male [méil]	男の				624
proper [prápər]	適切な				625
capable [kéipəbl]	〜する能力がある				626
independent [ìndɪpéndənt]	独立した				627
positive [pázitiv]	積極的な				628
pleasant [plézənt]	楽しい				629
significant [signífikənt]	重要な				630
former [fɔ́:rmər]	前の				631
chemical [kémikəl]	化学的な				632
upset [ʌpsét]	動揺している				633
previous [prí:viəs]	前の				634
calm [káːm]	冷静な				635
specific [spəsífik]	特定の				636
conscious [kánʃəs]	意識している				637
superior [supíəriər]	よりすぐれている				638
efficient [ifíʃənt]	効率がいい				639
fundamental [fʌndəméntəl]	基本的な				640
narrow [nǽrou]	狭い				641
reasonable [ríːznəbl]	理にかなった				642
nervous [nə́:rvəs]	神経質な				643
alike [əláik]	似ている				644
domestic [dəméstik]	家庭の				645
negative [négətiv]	否定の				646
moral [mɔ́(:)rəl]	道徳的な				647
eager [íːɡər]	熱心な				648
remarkable [rimáːrkəbl]	すばらしい				649
evil [íːvəl]	悪い				650

No.	英語フレーズ	フレーズ書きこみ	日本語フレーズ
651	stay awake all night		夜通し目が覚めている
652	his aged parents		彼の年老いた父母
653	I am anxious *about* your health.		君の健康が心配だ
654	a tough boxer		たくましいボクサー
655	nuclear energy		原子力エネルギー
656	the British legal system		イギリスの法律の制度
657	be curious *about* everything		何にでも好奇心を持つ
658	civil rights		市民権
659	according to a recent study		最近の研究によると
660	a senior member of the club		クラブの先輩の部員
661	Soon afterward, he left.		その後すぐ彼は去った
662	nearly 30 years ago		30年近く前に
663	The car is small and therefore cheap.		その車は小さい。それゆえ安い。
664	at exactly *the same* time		ぴったり同時に
665	He will possibly come.		ひょっとすると彼は来るかもしれない
666	contrary *to* expectations		予想に反して
667	I occasionally go to the theater.		私はたまに劇場に行く
668	Somehow I feel lonely.		なぜか寂しい
669	I seldom see him.		彼に会うことはめったにない
670	This is smaller and thus cheaper.		この方が小さく, したがって安い
671	people throughout the world		世界中の人々
672	Unlike my wife, I get up early.		妻と違って私は早起きだ
673	Besides being rich, he is kind.		彼は金持ちの上にやさしい
674	It's beyond my understanding.		私の理解をこえている
675	within a mile *of* the station		駅から1マイル以内で
676	have *neither* time nor money		時間もお金もない
677	I'll leave tomorrow unless it rains.		明日雨が降らない限り出発する
678	work *every* day except Sunday		日曜以外毎日働く
679	You ought *to* see a doctor.		君は医者に診てもらうべきだ
680	*in* spite *of* difficulties		困難にもかかわらず

単語	意味	書きこみ①	書きこみ②	書きこみ③	No.
awake [əwéik]	目を覚まして				651
aged [éidʒid]	年老いた				652
anxious [ǽŋkʃəs]	心配して				653
tough [tʌf]	たくましい				654
nuclear [njúːkliər]	核の				655
legal [líːgəl]	合法の				656
curious [kjúəriəs]	好奇心が強い				657
civil [sívl]	一般市民の				658
recent [ríːsnt]	最近の				659
senior [síːnjər]	上級の				660
afterward [ǽftərwərd]	その後				661
nearly [níərli]	ほとんど				662
therefore [ðéərfɔːr]	それゆえに				663
exactly [igzǽktli]	正確に				664
possibly [pásəbli]	ひょっとすると				665
contrary [kántreri]	反対に				666
occasionally [əkéiʒənəli]	時々				667
somehow [sʌmhau]	どういうわけか				668
seldom [séldəm]	めったに～ない				669
thus [ðʌs]	それゆえ				670
throughout [θru(ː)áut]	前～のいたる所に				671
unlike [ʌnláik]	前～と違って				672
besides [bisáidz]	前～に加えて				673
beyond [bijánd]	前～の向こうに				674
within [wiðín]	前以内で				675
nor [nɔ́ːr]	接～もない				676
unless [ənlés]	接～しない限り				677
except [iksépt]	前接～を除いて				678
ought to V [ɔ́ːt]	助Ｖすべきである				679
in spite of [spáit]	前～にもかかわらず				680

2 Fundamental

No.	英語フレーズ	フレーズ書きこみ	日本語フレーズ
681	I don't know whether it is true *or not*.		本当かどうかわからない
682	explain *why* he was late		彼がなぜ遅れたかを説明する
683	accept the truth as it is		ありのまま真実を受け入れる
684	produce enough food		十分な食料を生産する
685	Does God really exist?		神は本当に存在するのか
686	express my feelings		私の気持ちを表現する
687	add some milk *to* the soup		スープにミルクを加える
688	avoid mak*ing* mistakes		まちがいを犯すのを避ける
689	marry Mary		メアリと結婚する
690	protect children *from* danger		危険から子供たちを守る
691	Alcohol affects the brain.		アルコールは脳に影響する
692	determine your future		君の未来を決定する
693	solve the problem		問題を解決する
694	Vegetables contain a lot of water.		野菜はたくさんの水を含んでいる
695	discuss the problem with him		彼とその問題を議論する
696	ignore the doctor's advice		医者の忠告を無視する
697	guess how old she is		彼女の年を推測する
698	exchange yen *for* dollars		円をドルに交換する
699	satisfy the needs of students		学生の要求を満たす
700	complain *about* the noise		騒音のことで苦情を言う
701	finally achieve the goal		ついに目標を達成する
702	enable people *to* live longer		人々の長寿を可能にする
703	intend *to* live in America		アメリカに住むつもりだ
704	obtain information about him		彼に関する情報を得る
705	divide the cake *into* six pieces		ケーキを6個に分割する
706	The noise annoys me.		その音が私をいらだたせる
707	My opinion differs *from* hers.		私の考えは彼女と異なる
708	how to educate children		子供を教育する方法
709	borrow a book *from* a friend		友達から本を借りる
710	invent a time machine		タイムマシンを発明する

単語	意味	書きこみ①	書きこみ②	書きこみ③	No.
whether [hwéðər]	接 ～かどうか				681
explain [ikspléin]	～を説明する				682
accept [əksépt]	～を受け入れる				683
produce [prədjúːs]	～を生産する				684
exist [igzíst]	存在する				685
express [iksprés]	～を表現する				686
add [æd]	～を加える				687
avoid [əvɔ́id]	～を避ける				688
marry [mǽri]	～と結婚する				689
protect [prətékt]	～を守る				690
affect [əfékt]	～に影響する				691
determine [ditə́ːrmin]	～を決定する				692
solve [sálv]	～を解決する				693
contain [kəntéin]	～を含んでいる				694
discuss [diskʌ́s]	～を議論する				695
ignore [ignɔ́ːr]	～を無視する				696
guess [gés]	～を推測する				697
exchange [ikstʃéindʒ]	交換する				698
satisfy [sǽtisfai]	～を満たす				699
complain [kəmpléin]	苦情を言う				700
achieve [ətʃíːv]	～を達成する				701
enable [inéibl]	～を可能にする				702
intend [inténd]	～を意図する				703
obtain [əbtéin]	～を得る				704
divide [diváid]	分割する				705
annoy [ənɔ́i]	～をいらだたせる				706
differ [dífər]	異なる				707
educate [édʒukeit]	～を教育する				708
borrow [bárou]	～を借りる				709
invent [invént]	～を発明する				710

2

Fundamental

No.	英語フレーズ	フレーズ書きこみ	日本語フレーズ
711	promote economic growth		経済成長を促進する
712	advise him *to* eat vegetables		野菜を食べるよう彼に忠告する
713	retire *from* work at sixty		60で仕事を辞める
714	permit him *to* go out		彼に外出することを許す
715	recommend this book *to* you		あなたにこの本を勧める
716	apologize *to* him *for* being late		遅れたことを彼に謝る
717	inform him *of* his son's success		息子の成功を彼に知らせる
718	oppose their marriage		彼らの結婚に反対する
719	trust an old friend		古い友達を信用する
720	select the best answer		最良の答えを選ぶ
721	praise him *for* his work		仕事のことで彼をほめる
722	how to handle problems		どう問題に対処するべきか
723	propose a new way		新しいやり方を提案する
724	breathe fresh air		新鮮な空気を呼吸する
725	criticize him *for* being late		遅刻したことで彼を非難する
726	overcome difficulties		困難に打ち勝つ
727	possess great power		大きな力を持っている
728	predict the future		未来を予言する
729	publish a book		本を出版する
730	leaves floating on the river		川面に浮かぶ木の葉
731	recall the good old days		古き良き時代を思い出す
732	explore the Amazon River		アマゾン川を探検する
733	pretend *to* be asleep		眠っているふりをする
734	absorb a lot of water		大量の水を吸収する
735	He resembles his father.		彼は父親に似ている
736	tear the letter to pieces		ずたずたに手紙を引き裂く
737	consume a lot of energy		多量のエネルギーを消費する
738	compete *with* him *for* the gold medal		金メダルを目指して彼と競争する
739	quit smok*ing*		タバコをやめる
740	announce a new plan		新しい計画を発表する

単語	意味	書きこみ①	書きこみ②	書きこみ③	No.
promote [prəmóut]	〜を促進する				711
advise [ədváiz]	〜に忠告する				712
retire [ritáiər]	辞める				713
permit [pərmít]	〜を許す				714
recommend [rekəménd]	〜を勧める				715
apologize [əpálədʒaiz]	謝る				716
inform [infɔ́ːrm]	〜に知らせる				717
oppose [əpóuz]	〜に反対する				718
trust [trʌ́st]	〜を信用する				719
select [səlékt]	〜を選ぶ				720
praise [préiz]	〜をほめる				721
handle [hǽndl]	〜に対処する				722
propose [prəpóuz]	〜を提案する				723
breathe [bríːð]	〜を呼吸する				724
criticize [krítəsaiz]	〜を非難する				725
overcome [ouvərkʌ́m]	〜に打ち勝つ				726
possess [pəzés]	〜を持っている				727
predict [pridíkt]	〜を予言する				728
publish [pʌ́bliʃ]	〜を出版する				729
float [flóut]	浮かぶ				730
recall [rikɔ́ːl]	〜を思い出す				731
explore [iksplɔ́ːr]	〜を探検する				732
pretend [priténd]	ふりをする				733
absorb [əbzɔ́ːrb]	〜を吸収する				734
resemble [rizémbl]	〜に似ている				735
tear [téər]	〜を引き裂く				736
consume [kənsjúːm]	〜を消費する				737
compete [kəmpíːt]	競争する				738
quit [kwít]	〜をやめる				739
announce [ənáuns]	〜を発表する				740

2
Fundamental

No.	英語フレーズ	フレーズ書きこみ	日本語フレーズ
741	react quickly *to* light		光にすばやく反応する
742	wander around the streets		街を歩き回る
743	Don't text while driving.		運転中にメールを送るな
744	generate electricity		電力を生み出す
745	score 10 goals		10点を取る
746	the Japanese government		日本政府
747	have little knowledge of English		英語の知識がほとんどない
748	the Asian nations		アジアの諸国
749	*make* an effort *to* help him		彼を助けようと努力する
750	the Cold War period		冷戦時代
751	population growth		人口の増加
752	*for* peaceful purposes		平和的な目的で
753	study human behavior		人間の行動を研究する
754	lack of food		食糧不足
755	learn basic skills		基本的な技術を学ぶ
756	the sound quality of the CD		CDの音質
757	*the* natural environment		自然環境
758	*play* an important role		重要な役割を果たす
759	a positive attitude *toward* life		人生に対する前向きな態度
760	the author of this passage		この文章の筆者
761	scientific research		科学的な研究
762	an opportunity *to* talk to her		彼女と話す機会
763	a source of information		情報源
764	carbon dioxide		二酸化炭素
765	the shape of her nose		彼女の鼻の形
766	the advantage *of* membership		会員の利点
767	a method of teaching English		英語を教える方法
768	be in the habit of reading in bed		ベッドで本を読む習慣がある
769	remember the details of the story		話を細部まで覚えている
770	within walking distance of my house		私の家から歩ける距離で

単語	意味	書きこみ①	書きこみ②	書きこみ③	No.
react [ri(:)ækt]	反応する				741
wander [wάndər]	歩き回る				742
text [tékst]	メールを送る				743
generate [dʒénəreit]	～を生み出す				744
score [skɔ́ːr]	～を取る				745
government [gʌ́vərnmənt]	政府				746
knowledge [nάlidʒ]	知識				747
nation [néiʃən]	国				748
effort [éfərt]	努力				749
period [píəriəd]	時代				750
population [pɑpjuléiʃən]	人口				751
purpose [pɔ́ːrpəs]	目的				752
behavior [bihéivjər]	行動				753
lack [lǽk]	不足				754
skill [skíl]	技術				755
quality [kwάləti]	質				756
environment [invάiərənmənt]	環境				757
role [róul]	役割				758
attitude [ǽtitjuːd]	態度				759
author [ɔ́ːθər]	筆者				760
research [rísəːrtʃ]	研究				761
opportunity [ɑpərtjúnəti]	機会				762
source [sɔ́ːrs]	源				763
carbon [kάːrbən]	炭素				764
shape [ʃéip]	形				765
advantage [ədvǽntidʒ]	利点				766
method [méθəd]	方法				767
habit [hǽbit]	習慣				768
detail [díːteil]	細部				769
distance [dístəns]	距離				770

2 Fundamental

No.	英語フレーズ	フレーズ書きこみ	日本語フレーズ
771	A large crowd gathered.		大群衆が集まった
772	the best known instance		最もよく知られた例
773	a strong desire *to* be a singer		歌手になりたいという強い願望
774	the standard of living		生活水準
775	a difficult task		難しい仕事
776	for future generations		未来の世代のために
777	*take* responsibility *for* the accident		事故の責任をとる
778	experiments with animals		動物を用いる実験
779	a professional athlete		プロの運動選手
780	only a decade ago		ほんの10年前に
781	a loss of $5,000		5,000ドルの損失
782	have a high fever		高熱を出している
783	the theory of relativity		相対性理論
784	read the following statement		次の記述を読む
785	a professor at Boston University		ボストン大学の教授
786	the basic functions of a computer		コンピュータの基本的機能
787	the surface of the earth		地球の表面
788	put the letter in a pink envelope		ピンクの封筒に手紙を入れる
789	an international organization		国際的な組織
790	Japan's foreign policy		日本の外交政策
791	natural resources		天然資源
792	the contrast between light and shadow		光と影の対比
793	a flood of information		情報の洪水
794	look for a mate		連れ合いを探す
795	buying and selling goods		商品の売り買い
796	humans and other creatures		人間と他の動物
797	changes in social structure		社会構造の変化
798	history and tradition		歴史と伝統
799	lose weight		体重を減らす
800	give money to charity		慈善のために寄付する

単語	意味	書きこみ①	書きこみ②	書きこみ③	No.
crowd [kráud]	群衆				771
instance [ínstəns]	例				772
desire [dizáiər]	願望				773
standard [stǽndərd]	水準				774
task [tǽsk]	仕事				775
generation [dʒenəréiʃən]	世代				776
responsibility [rispɑnsəbíləti]	責任				777
experiment [ikspérimənt]	実験				778
athlete [ǽθliːt]	運動選手				779
decade [dékeid]	10年				780
loss [lɔ́(ː)s]	損失				781
fever [fíːvər]	熱				782
theory [θíəri]	理論				783
statement [stéitmənt]	記述				784
professor [prəfésər]	教授				785
function [fʌ́ŋkʃən]	機能				786
surface [sə́ːrfis]	表面				787
envelope [énvəloup]	封筒				788
organization [ɔːrɡənizéiʃən]	組織				789
policy [pɑ́lisi]	政策				790
resource [ríːsɔːrs]	資源				791
contrast [kɑ́ntræst] 動 [kəntrǽst]	対比				792
flood [flʌ́d]	洪水				793
mate [méit]	連れ合い				794
goods [ɡúdz]	商品				795
creature [kríːtʃər]	動物				796
structure [strʌ́ktʃər]	構造				797
tradition [trədíʃən]	伝統				798
weight [wéit]	体重				799
charity [tʃǽrəti]	慈善				800

2 Fundamental

No.	英語フレーズ	フレーズ書きこみ	日本語フレーズ
801	the average American citizen		平均的アメリカ市民
802	*make* a good impression *on* him		彼によい印象を与える
803	a popular cartoon character		人気マンガのキャラクター
804	a long career as an actress		女優としての長い経歴
805	a site for a new hotel		新しいホテルの用地
806	train passengers		列車の乗客
807	violence on TV		テレビにおける暴力
808	low-income families		低所得の家族
809	the average temperature in Paris		パリの平均気温
810	*the* majority *of* students		大多数の学生
811	the origin of language		言語の起源
812	study English literature		英文学を研究する
813	office equipment		オフィスの設備
814	talk to a stranger		見知らぬ人に話しかける
815	strength and weakness		強さと弱さ
816	the planet Earth		地球という惑星
817	Truth is stranger than fiction.		事実は小説よりも奇なり
818	science and religion		科学と宗教
819	environmental pollution		環境汚染
820	wealth and power		富と権力
821	sign an official document		公文書にサインする
822	make a $2 million profit		200万ドルのもうけを得る
823	the technique of film-making		映画作りの技術
824	express emotions		感情を表現する
825	a natural phenomenon		自然現象
826	a horror movie		恐怖映画
827	climb a ladder		はしごを登る
828	8 billion people		八十億の人々
829	the social status of women		女性の社会的地位
830	modern youth		現代の若者

単語	意味	書きこみ①	書きこみ②	書きこみ③	No.
citizen [sítizn]	市民				801
impression [impréʃən]	印象				802
cartoon [kɑːrtúːn]	マンガ				803
career [kəríər]	経歴				804
site [sáit]	用地				805
passenger [pǽsendʒər]	乗客				806
violence [váiələns]	暴力				807
income [ínkʌm]	所得				808
temperature [témpərətʃər]	気温				809
majority [mədʒɔ́(ː)rəti]	大多数				810
origin [ɔ́(ː)ridʒin]	起源				811
literature [lítərətʃər]	文学				812
equipment [ikwípmənt]	設備				813
stranger [stréindʒər]	見知らぬ人				814
strength [stréŋkθ]	強さ				815
planet [plǽnit]	惑星				816
fiction [fíkʃən]	小説				817
religion [rilídʒən]	宗教				818
pollution [pəljúːʃən]	汚染				819
wealth [wélθ]	富				820
document [dákjumənt]	文書				821
profit [práfit]	もうけ				822
technique [tekníːk]	技術				823
emotion [imóuʃən]	感情				824
phenomenon [finámənɑn]	現象				825
horror [hɔ́(ː)rər]	恐怖				826
ladder [lǽdər]	はしご				827
billion [bíljən]	十億				828
status [stéitəs]	地位				829
youth [júːθ]	若者				830

2 Fundamental

No.	英語フレーズ	フレーズ書きこみ	日本語フレーズ
831	have confidence *in* my ability		自分の能力に自信がある
832	the edge of the Pacific Ocean		太平洋の周辺
833	household goods		家庭用品
834	a great scholar		偉大な学者
835	according to a new survey		新しい調査によると
836	a vocabulary of 5,000 words		5,000語の語彙
837	a natural enemy		天敵
838	a bridge *under* construction		建設中の橋
839	a lecture *on* history		歴史に関する講義
840	follow his instructions		彼の指示に従う
841	get over the economic crisis		経済危機を乗り越える
842	a dentist's instrument		歯医者の道具
843	grow various crops		さまざまな作物を育てる
844	a laser weapon		レーザー兵器
845	an electronic device		電子装置
846	the path *to* victory		勝利への道
847	predict earthquakes		地震を予知する
848	a clear mountain stream		きれいな山の小川
849	the notion of freedom		自由の概念
850	a tree in the yard		庭の木
851	victims of the war		戦争の犠牲者
852	run out of fuel		燃料を使い果たす
853	the common ancestors of all humans		すべての人類の共通の祖先
854	the rich soil of the Nile River		ナイル川の豊かな土壌
855	a debate on education		教育についての討論
856	a violent crime		凶悪犯罪
857	my friends and colleagues		私の友人と同僚
858	take a book from the shelf		たなから本を取る
859	analysis *of* DNA		DNAの分析
860	stars in the universe		宇宙の星

単語	意味	書きこみ①	書きこみ②	書きこみ③	No.
confidence [kánfidəns]	自信				831
edge [édʒ]	周辺				832
household [háushould]	家庭				833
scholar [skálər]	学者				834
survey [sə́ːrvei] 動 [səːrvéi]	調査				835
vocabulary [voukǽbjəleri]	語彙				836
enemy [énəmi]	敵				837
construction [kənstrʌ́kʃən]	建設				838
lecture [léktʃər]	講義				839
instruction [instrʌ́kʃən]	指示				840
crisis [kráisis]	危機				841
instrument [ínstrəmənt]	道具				842
crop [krάp]	作物				843
weapon [wépən]	兵器				844
device [diváis]	装置				845
path [pǽθ]	道				846
earthquake [ə́ːrθkweik]	地震				847
stream [stríːm]	小川				848
notion [nóuʃən]	概念				849
yard [jάːrd]	庭				850
victim [víktim]	犠牲者				851
fuel [fjú(ː)əl]	燃料				852
ancestor [ǽnsestər]	祖先				853
soil [sɔ́il]	土壌				854
debate [dibéit]	討論				855
crime [kráim]	犯罪				856
colleague [káliːg]	同僚				857
shelf [ʃélf]	たな				858
analysis [ənǽlisis]	分析				859
universe [júːnəvəːrs]	宇宙				860

2 Fundamental

No.	英語フレーズ	フレーズ書きこみ	日本語フレーズ
861	a machine run by electricity		電気で動く機械
862	social insects like ants		アリのような社会性昆虫
863	be caught in a spider's web		クモの巣にかかる
864	a heavy storm		激しい嵐
865	have plenty _of_ time		十分な時間がある
866	land suitable for agriculture		農業に向いた土地
867	the gene for eye color		目の色を決める遺伝子
868	evidence of life on Mars		火星に生物がいるという証拠
869	_have_ serious consequences		重大な結果をまねく
870	the mother-infant relationship		母親と幼児の関係
871	have no leisure time for sports		スポーツをする暇がない
872	the gray cells of the brain		灰色の脳細胞
873	have musical talent		音楽の才能がある
874	newspaper advertising		新聞広告
875	increase _to_ some extent		ある程度まで増える
876	take out the garbage		ゴミを出す
877	the general public		一般大衆
878	various kinds of flowers		さまざまな種類の花
879	be similar _to_ each other		お互いに似ている
880	a complete failure		完全な失敗
881	a sharp rise in prices		物価の急激な上昇
882	an expensive restaurant		高価なレストラン
883	a political leader		政治的な指導者
884	be aware _of_ the danger		危険に気づいている
885	ancient Greece and Rome		古代のギリシャとローマ
886	a medical study		医学の研究
887	Water is essential _to_ life.		水は生命に不可欠だ
888	a huge city		巨大な都市
889	a terrible accident		ひどい事故
890	practical English		実用的な英語

単語	意味	書きこみ①	書きこみ②	書きこみ③	No.
electricity [ilektrísəti]	電気				861
insect [ínsekt]	昆虫				862
web [wéb]	巣				863
storm [stɔ́ːrm]	嵐				864
plenty [plénti]	十分				865
agriculture [ǽɡrikʌltʃər]	農業				866
gene [dʒíːn]	遺伝子				867
evidence [évidəns]	証拠				868
consequence [kánsikwens]	結果				869
infant [ínfənt]	幼児				870
leisure [líːʒər]	暇				871
cell [sél]	細胞				872
talent [tǽlənt]	才能				873
advertising [ǽdvərtaiziŋ]	広告				874
extent [ikstént]	程度				875
garbage [ɡáːrbidʒ]	ゴミ				876
general [dʒénərəl]	一般の				877
various [véəriəs]	さまざまな				878
similar [símələr]	似ている				879
complete [kəmplíːt]	完全な				880
sharp [ʃáːrp]	急激な				881
expensive [ikspénsiv]	高価な				882
political [pəlítikəl]	政治的な				883
aware [əwéər]	気づいている				884
ancient [éinʃənt]	古代の				885
medical [médikəl]	医学の				886
essential [isénʃəl]	不可欠な				887
huge [hjúːdʒ]	巨大な				888
terrible [térəbl]	ひどい				889
practical [prǽktikəl]	実用的な				890

2 Fundamental

No.	英語フレーズ	フレーズ書きこみ	日本語フレーズ
891	the entire world		全世界
892	my favorite food		私のいちばん好きな食べ物
893	enjoy a comfortable life		快適な生活を楽しむ
894	a minor problem		小さい問題
895	a typical American family		典型的なアメリカの家族
896	an ideal place to live		生活するのに理想的な土地
897	the principal cities of Europe		ヨーロッパの主要な都市
898	the most appropriate word		最も適切な単語
899	an empty bottle		からのビン
900	rapid economic growth		急速な経済成長
901	a mental illness		精神の病
902	an excellent idea		すばらしいアイディア
903	when it's convenient _for_ you		君の都合がいいときに
904	potential danger		潜在的な危険
905	financial support from the US		アメリカからの財政的援助
906	an enormous amount of damage		ばく大な額の損害
907	a rare stamp		珍しい切手
908	artificial intelligence		人工知能 (AI)
909	a tiny kitten		ちっちゃな子猫
910	spend considerable time		かなりの時間を費やす
911	Her skin is sensitive _to_ sunlight.		彼女の肌は日光に敏感だ
912	high intellectual ability		高度な知的能力
913	Salty food makes you thirsty.		塩分の多い食事でのどが渇く
914	be polite to ladies		女性に対して礼儀正しい
915	accurate information		正確な情報
916	rude behavior		失礼な振る舞い
917	pay sufficient attention		十分な注意を払う
918	urban life		都会の暮らし
919	temporary loss of memory		一時的な記憶喪失
920	a primitive society		原始的な社会

単語	意味	書きこみ①	書きこみ②	書きこみ③	No.
entire [intáiər]	全体の				891
favorite [féivərət]	いちばん好きな				892
comfortable [kʌ́mfərtəbl]	快適な				893
minor [máinər]	小さい				894
typical [típikl]	典型的な				895
ideal [aidíːəl]	理想的な				896
principal [prínsəpl]	主要な				897
appropriate [əpróupriət]	適切な				898
empty [émpti]	からの				899
rapid [rǽpid]	急速な				900
mental [méntəl]	精神の				901
excellent [éksələnt]	すばらしい				902
convenient [kənvíːniənt]	都合がいい				903
potential [pəténʃəl]	潜在的な				904
financial [fainǽnʃəl]	財政的な				905
enormous [inɔ́ːrməs]	ばく大な				906
rare [réər]	珍しい				907
artificial [ɑːrtəfíʃəl]	人工の				908
tiny [táini]	ちっちゃな				909
considerable [kənsídərəbl]	かなりの				910
sensitive [sénsətiv]	敏感な				911
intellectual [intəléktʃuəl]	知的な				912
thirsty [θɔ́ːrsti]	のどが渇く				913
politc [pəláit]	礼儀正しい				914
accurate [ǽkjərət]	正確な				915
rude [rúːd]	失礼な				916
sufficient [səfíʃənt]	十分な				917
urban [ɔ́ːrbən]	都会の				918
temporary [témpəreri]	一時的な				919
primitive [prímətiv]	原始的な				920

2
Fundamental

No.	英語フレーズ	フレーズ書きこみ	日本語フレーズ
921	permanent teeth		永久歯
922	the care of elderly people		高齢者のケア
923	severe winter weather		厳しい冬の天候
924	a brief explanation		簡潔な説明
925	a mobile society		流動的な社会
926	the latest news from China		中国からの最新のニュース
927	military aid to Israel		イスラエルへの軍事的援助
928	strict rules		厳しい規則
929	a solid state		固体の状態
930	say stupid things		ばかなことを言う
931	biological weapons		生物兵器
932	Probably he won't come.		おそらく彼は来ないだろう
933	I hardly know Bill.		ビルのことはほとんど知らない
934	leave immediately after lunch		昼食後すぐに出発する
935	He eventually became president.		ついに彼は大統領になった
936	a frequently used word		しばしば使われる言葉
937	an extremely difficult problem		非常に難しい問題
938	gradually become colder		だんだん冷たくなる
939	instantly recognizable songs		すぐにそれとわかる歌
940	He is rich; nevertheless he is unhappy.		彼は金持ちだが, それにもかかわらず, 不幸だ
941	He's kind; moreover, he's strong.		彼は親切で, その上強い
942	relatively few people		比較的少数の人々
943	an apparently simple question		一見簡単な問題
944	I will definitely not marry you.		絶対あなたとは結婚しない
945	largely because of the problem		主にその問題のせいで
946	The class is mostly Japanese.		クラスの大部分は日本人だ
947	approximately 10,000 years ago		およそ1万年前
948	stay overnight in his house		彼の家で一晩泊まる
949	accidentally discover an island		偶然島を発見する
950	He lost despite his efforts.		努力にもかかわらず彼は負けた

単語	意味	書きこみ①	書きこみ②	書きこみ③	No.
permanent [pə́:rmənənt]	永久の				921
elderly [éldərli]	高齢の				922
severe [sivíər]	厳しい				923
brief [brí:f]	簡潔な				924
mobile [móubəl]	流動的な				925
latest [léitist]	最新の				926
military [míləteri]	軍事的な				927
strict [stríkt]	厳しい				928
solid [sálid]	固体の				929
stupid [stjú:pid]	ばかな				930
biological [baiəládʒikəl]	生物の				931
probably [prábəbli]	おそらく				932
hardly [há:rdli]	ほとんど～ない				933
immediately [imí:diətli]	すぐに				934
eventually [ivéntʃuəli]	ついに				935
frequently [frí:kwəntli]	しばしば				936
extremely [ikstrí:mli]	非常に				937
gradually [grǽdʒuəli]	だんだん				938
instantly [ínstəntli]	すぐに				939
nevertheless [nevərðəlés]	それにもかかわらず				940
moreover [mɔːróuvər]	その上				941
relatively [rélətivli]	比較的				942
apparently [əpǽrəntli]	一見				943
definitely [définətli]	絶対に				944
largely [lá:rdʒli]	主に				945
mostly [móustli]	大部分は				946
approximately [əpráksəmətli]	およそ				947
overnight [óuvərnáit]	一晩中				948
accidentally [æksidéntli]	偶然に				949
despite [dispáit]	前 ～にもかかわらず				950

2

Fundamental

Stage 3

Essential Stage

"In the middle of difficulty lies opportunity"
—— *Albert Einstein*

*　*　*

困難の中にチャンスがある。
—アルバート・アインシュタイン

No.	英語フレーズ	フレーズ書きこみ	日本語フレーズ
951	proceed straight ahead		まっすぐ前に進む
952	ensure the safety of drivers		ドライバーの安全を確保する
953	interpret the meaning of the word		その言葉の意味を解釈する
954	Some countries ceased _to_ exist.		いくつかの国は存在しなくなった
955	ban smoking in public places		公共の場の喫煙を禁ずる
956	obey the law		法に従う
957	eliminate the need for paper		紙の必要性をなくす
958	resist pressure from above		上からの圧力に抵抗する
959	accompany the president		大統領に同伴する
960	commit a crime		犯罪を犯す
961	pursue the American Dream		アメリカンドリームを追い求める
962	demonstrate _that_ it is impossible		それが不可能なことを示す
963	I bet you'll win.		きっと君は勝つと思う
964	ruin his life		彼の人生を破滅させる
965	threaten _to_ tell the police		警察に言うとおどす
966	a bookcase attached _to_ the wall		壁に取り付けられた本棚
967	reverse the positions		立場を逆転する
968	restrict freedom of speech		言論の自由を制限する
969	The body is composed _of_ cells.		体は細胞で構成されている
970	lean against the wall		壁にもたれる
971	substitute margarine _for_ butter		マーガリンをバターの代わりに用いる
972	trace human history		人類の歴史をたどる
973	interrupt their conversation		彼らの会話をじゃまする
974	confront a difficult problem		困難な問題に立ち向かう
975	This example illustrates his ability.		この例が彼の能力を示す
976	arrest him _for_ speeding		スピード違反で彼を逮捕する
977	stimulate the imagination		想像力を刺激する
978	assure you _that_ you will win		君が勝つことを保証する
979	consult a doctor for advice		医者に相談して助言を求める
980	feel too depressed to go out		憂鬱で出かける気がしない

単語	意味	書きこみ①	書きこみ②	書きこみ③	No.
proceed [prəsíːd]	進む				951
ensure [inʃúər]	～を確実にする				952
interpret [intə́ːrprit]	～を解釈する				953
cease to V [síːs]	Vしなくなる				954
ban [bǽn]	～を禁止する				955
obey [oubéi]	～に従う				956
eliminate [ilímineit]	～を除去する				957
resist [rizíst]	～に抵抗する				958
accompany [əkʌ́mpəni]	～に同伴する				959
commit [kəmít]	～を犯す				960
pursue [pərsjúː]	～を追求する				961
demonstrate [démənstreit]	～を明らかに示す				962
bet [bét]	きっと～だと思う				963
ruin [rúːin]	～を台無しにする				964
threaten [θrétn]	～を脅迫する				965
attach A to B [ətǽtʃ]	AをBにくっつける				966
reverse [rivə́ːrs]	～を反対にする				967
restrict [ristríkt]	～を制限する				968
compose [kəmpóuz]	～を組み立てる				969
lean [líːn]	寄りかかる				970
substitute [sʌ́bstətjuːt]	～を代わりに用いる				971
trace [tréis]	～の跡をたどる				972
interrupt [intərʌ́pt]	～を妨げる				973
confront [kənfrʌ́nt]	～の前に立ちふさがる				974
illustrate [íləstreit]	～を示す				975
arrest [ərést]	～を逮捕する				976
stimulate [stímjəleit]	～を刺激する				977
assure [əʃúər]	（～を）保証する				978
consult [kənsʌ́lt]	～に相談する				979
depress [diprés]	～を憂鬱にさせる				980

3

Essential

No.	英語フレーズ	フレーズ書きこみ	日本語フレーズ
981 ☐	crash *into* the wall		壁に激突する
982 ☐	inspire him *to* write a poem		彼に詩を書く気を起こさせる
983 ☐	specialize *in* Chinese history		中国史を専攻する
984 ☐	cultivate plants		植物を栽培する
985 ☐	fulfill the promise		約束を果たす
986 ☐	transmit messages		メッセージを伝える
987 ☐	found a computer company		コンピュータ会社を設立する
988 ☐	Clap your hands as you sing.		歌いながら手をたたきなさい
989 ☐	burst *into* tears		急に泣き出す
990 ☐	bow *to* the queen		女王様におじぎする
991 ☐	dismiss the idea *as* nonsense		その考えをばからしいと無視する
992 ☐	how to breed animals		動物を繁殖させる方法
993 ☐	prohibit children *from* working		子供が働くのを禁じる
994 ☐	*be* obliged *to* pay the price		対価を支払わざるをえない
995 ☐	qualify *for* the position		その地位に適任である
996 ☐	invest money *in* a business		ビジネスにお金を投資する
997 ☐	grasp what he is saying		彼の言うことを理解する
998 ☐	The building collapsed.		建物が崩壊した
999 ☐	overlook the fact		事実を見逃す
1000 ☐	accuse him *of* lying		彼がうそをついたと非難する
1001 ☐	be frustrated by the lack of money		金がなくて欲求不満になる
1002 ☐	deprive him *of* the chance		彼からチャンスを奪う
1003 ☐	an astonishing memory		驚異的な記憶力
1004 ☐	register a new car		新車を登録する
1005 ☐	The fact corresponds *to* my theory.		その事実は私の理論と一致する
1006 ☐	cast a shadow on the wall		壁に影を投げかける
1007 ☐	attribute success *to* luck		成功は幸運のおかげだと思う
1008 ☐	neglect human rights		人権を無視する
1009 ☐	feed starving children		飢えた子どもたちに食事を与える
1010 ☐	resolve disagreements		意見の不一致を解決する

単語	意味	書きこみ①	書きこみ②	書きこみ③	No.
crash [krǽʃ]	激突する				981
inspire [inspáiər]	〜を奮起させる				982
specialize in A [spéʃəlaiz]	Aを専門にする				983
cultivate [kʌ́ltəveit]	〜を栽培する				984
fulfill [fulfíl]	〜を果たす				985
transmit [trænsmít]	〜を送る				986
found [fáund]	〜を創立する				987
clap [klǽp]	〜をたたく				988
burst [bɔ́ːrst]	破裂する				989
bow [báu]	おじぎする				990
dismiss [dismís]	〜を無視する				991
breed [bríːd]	〜を繁殖させる				992
prohibit [prouhíbət]	〜を禁じる				993
oblige [əbláidʒ]	〜に強いる				994
qualify for A [kwáləfai]	Aに適任である				995
invest [invést]	投資する				996
grasp [grǽsp]	〜を理解する				997
collapse [kəlǽps]	崩壊する				998
overlook [ouvərlúk]	〜を見落とす				999
accuse [əkjúːz]	〜を非難する				1000
frustrate [frʌ́streit]	〜を欲求不満にさせる				1001
deprive A of B [dipráiv]	AからBを奪う				1002
astonish [əstániʃ]	〜を驚嘆させる				1003
register [rédʒistər]	〜を登録する				1004
correspond [kɔrəspánd]	一致する				1005
cast [kǽst]	〜を投げる				1006
attribute A to B [ətríbjuːt] 名 [ǽtribjuːt]	AをBのおかげだと思う				1007
neglect [niglékt]	〜を無視する				1008
starve [stáːrv]	飢える				1009
resolve [rizálv]	〜を解決する				1010

3

Essential

No.	英語フレーズ	フレーズ書きこみ	日本語フレーズ
1011	impose rules *on* students		学生に規則を押しつける
1012	convert sunlight *into* electricity		太陽の光を電気に転換する
1013	The noise scares him.		その音が彼をおびえさせる
1014	Cars constitute 10% of exports.		車が輸出の10%を占める
1015	*be* appointed *to* an important post		重要なポストに任命される
1016	What does her smile imply?		彼女の微笑みは何を意味するのか
1017	assign work *to* each member		各メンバーに仕事を割り当てる
1018	nod and say "yes"		うなずいて「はい」と言う
1019	*be* elected president		大統領に選ばれる
1020	He was transferred *to* Osaka.		彼は大阪に転勤した
1021	rob the bank *of* $50,000		銀行から5万ドル奪う
1022	capture wild animals		野生動物を捕らえる
1023	undertake the work		仕事を引き受ける
1024	save a drowning child		おぼれている子供を救う
1025	split into two groups		2つのグループに分裂する
1026	resort *to* violence		暴力に訴える
1027	descend to the ground		地面に降りる
1028	irritating noise		いらいらさせる騒音
1029	pronounce the word correctly		正確にその単語を発音する
1030	The car is equipped *with* AI.		その車はAIが装備されている
1031	cheat consumers		消費者をだます
1032	A new problem has emerged.		新たな問題が出現した
1033	He devoted *himself to* his work.		彼は仕事に身をささげた
1034	Time heals all wounds.		時はすべての傷をいやす
1035	urge him *to* go home		帰宅するよう彼を説得する
1036	envy the rich		金持ちをうらやむ
1037	chase the car		その車を追跡する
1038	prompt him to speak		彼に話をするよう促す
1039	withdraw my hand		手を引っ込める
1040	how to detect lies		うそを発見する方法

単語	意味	書きこみ①	書きこみ②	書きこみ③	No.
impose A on B [impóuz]	AをBに課す				1011
convert [kənvə́ːrt]	〜を転換する				1012
scare [skéər]	〜をおびえさせる				1013
constitute [kánstətjuːt]	〜を構成する				1014
appoint [əpɔ́int]	〜を任命する				1015
imply [implái]	〜を意味する				1016
assign [əsáin]	〜を割り当てる				1017
nod [nád]	うなずく				1018
elect [ilékt]	〜を選挙で選ぶ				1019
transfer [trænsfə́ːr]	〜を移す				1020
rob A of B [ráb]	AからBを奪う				1021
capture [kǽptʃər]	〜を捕らえる				1022
undertake [ʌndərtéik]	〜を引き受ける				1023
drown [dráun]	おぼれ死ぬ				1024
split [splít]	〜を割る				1025
resort to A [rizɔ́ːrt]	Aに訴える				1026
descend [disénd]	下る				1027
irritate [íriteit]	〜をいらだたせる				1028
pronounce [prənáuns]	〜を発音する				1029
equip [ikwíp]	〜を装備させる				1030
cheat [tʃíːt]	いかさまをする				1031
emerge [imə́ːrdʒ]	現れる				1032
devote [divóut]	〜をささげる				1033
heal [híːl]	〜を治す				1034
urge [ə́ːrdʒ]	〜に強く迫る				1035
envy [énvi]	〜をうらやむ				1036
chase [tʃéis]	〜を追いかける				1037
prompt [prámpt]	〜を促す				1038
withdraw [wiðdrɔ́ː]	〜を引っ込める				1039
detect [ditékt]	〜を探知する				1040

3

Essential

No.	英語フレーズ	フレーズ書きこみ	日本語フレーズ
1041	interfere *with* his work		彼の仕事をじゃまする
1042	You must be kidding.		冗談でしょう
1043	launch a space shuttle		スペースシャトルを発射する
1044	an endangered species		絶滅危惧種
1045	foster creativity		創造性を養う
1046	His power diminished.		彼の力は衰えた
1047	spill coffee on the keyboard		キーボードにコーヒーをこぼす
1048	be infected *with* the virus		ウイルスに感染している
1049	stem *from* an ancient tradition		古い伝統に由来する
1050	tap her on the shoulder		彼女の肩を軽くたたく
1051	embrace a new idea		新しい考えを受け入れる
1052	the proportion of boys *to* girls		男子と女子の比率
1053	sign a contract *with* Google		グーグルとの契約にサインする
1054	have chest pains		胸が痛む
1055	discover treasure		財宝を発見する
1056	the Tokyo stock market		東京株式市場
1057	public facilities		公共施設
1058	a large sum of money		多額のお金
1059	a man of high rank		高い地位の人
1060	a modern democracy		近代民主国家
1061	an emergency room		救急治療室
1062	a protest *against* war		戦争に対する抗議
1063	immigrants from Mexico		メキシコからの移民
1064	a vehicle for communication		意思伝達の手段
1065	a healthy daily routine		健康的ないつもの日課
1066	write really good stuff		本当によいものを書く
1067	sit in the front row		最前列に座る
1068	your online profile		君のオンラインのプロフィール
1069	leave home *at* dawn		夜明けに家を出る
1070	social welfare		社会福祉

単語	意味	書きこみ①	書きこみ②	書きこみ③	No.
interfere with A [intərfíər]	Aをじゃまする				1041
kid [kíd]	冗談を言う				1042
launch [lɔ́:ntʃ]	〜を打ち上げる				1043
endanger [endéindʒər]	〜を危険にさらす				1044
foster [fɔ́(:)stər]	〜を促進する				1045
diminish [dimíniʃ]	減少する				1046
spill [spíl]	〜をこぼす				1047
infect [infékt]	〜に感染する				1048
stem from A [stém]	Aから生じる				1049
tap [tǽp]	〜を軽くたたく				1050
embrace [imbréis]	〜を受け入れる				1051
proportion [prəpɔ́:rʃən]	比率				1052
contract [kántrækt] 動 [─ ´]	契約				1053
chest [tʃést]	胸				1054
treasure [tréʒər]	財宝				1055
stock [sták]	株 (式)				1056
facility [fəsíləti]	設備				1057
sum [sʌ́m]	金額				1058
rank [rǽŋk]	地位				1059
democracy [dimákrəsi]	民主主義				1060
emergency [imɔ́:rdʒənsi]	緊急事態				1061
protest [próutest] 動 [prətést]	抗議				1062
immigrant [ímigrənt]	移民				1063
vehicle [ví:əkl]	車				1064
routine [ru:tí:n]	決まりきった仕事				1065
stuff [stʌ́f]	物				1066
row [róu]	列				1067
profile [próufail]	プロフィール				1068
dawn [dɔ́:n]	夜明け				1069
welfare [wélfeər]	福祉				1070

3

Essential

No.	英語フレーズ	フレーズ書きこみ	日本語フレーズ
1071 ☐	see life *from* a new perspective		新しい見方で人生を考える
1072 ☐	his enthusiasm *for* soccer		彼のサッカーに対する情熱
1073 ☐	have faith *in* technology		技術を信頼する
1074 ☐	a well-paid occupation		給料のよい職業
1075 ☐	a witness to the accident		事故の目撃者
1076 ☐	the kingdom of Denmark		デンマーク王国
1077 ☐	There's no English equivalent *to* haiku.		俳句に相当するものは英語にない
1078 ☐	achieve the objective		目標を達成する
1079 ☐	put the plates in a pile		皿を積み重ねて置く
1080 ☐	find shelter *from* the cold		寒さから逃れる場所を見つける
1081 ☐	trial and error		試行錯誤
1082 ☐	It's a great honor to work here.		ここで働けるのは大変名誉です
1083 ☐	defend a territory		なわ張りを守る
1084 ☐	a window frame		窓わく
1085 ☐	cross the Russian border		ロシア国境を越える
1086 ☐	according to official statistics		公式の統計によると
1087 ☐	a private enterprise		民間企業
1088 ☐	the meaning *in* this context		この文脈における意味
1089 ☐	carry a heavy load		重い荷物を運ぶ
1090 ☐	world grain production		世界の穀物生産高
1091 ☐	a review of the law		その法律の再検討
1092 ☐	prejudice against women		女性に対する偏見
1093 ☐	put a strain *on* the heart		心臓に負担をかける
1094 ☐	fall into a trap		わなにはまる
1095 ☐	have a quick temper		すぐかっとなる気性である
1096 ☐	a black slave		黒人の奴隷
1097 ☐	a knife wound		ナイフの傷
1098 ☐	an increase in the divorce rate		離婚率の増加
1099 ☐	the beauty of the tune		その曲の美しさ
1100 ☐	Summer is *at* its height.		夏真っ盛りだ

単語	意味	書きこみ①	書きこみ②	書きこみ③	No.
perspective [pərspéktiv]	見方				1071
enthusiasm [inθjúːziæzm]	熱意				1072
faith [féiθ]	信頼				1073
occupation [ɑkjəpéiʃən]	職業				1074
witness [wítnəs]	証人				1075
kingdom [kíŋdəm]	王国				1076
equivalent [ikwívələnt]	同等のもの				1077
objective [əbdʒéktiv]	目的				1078
pile [páil]	積み重ね				1079
shelter [ʃéltər]	避難(所)				1080
trial [tráiəl]	試み				1081
honor [ánər]	名誉				1082
territory [térətɔːri]	領土				1083
frame [fréim]	わく				1084
border [bɔ́ːrdər]	国境地帯				1085
statistics [stətístiks]	統計(学)				1086
enterprise [éntərpraiz]	企業				1087
context [kántekst]	文脈				1088
load [lóud]	荷物				1089
grain [gréin]	穀物				1090
review [rivjúː]	再検討				1091
prejudice [prédʒədəs]	偏見				1092
strain [stréin]	負担				1093
trap [trǽp]	わな				1094
temper [témpər]	気性				1095
slave [sléiv]	奴隷				1096
wound [wúːnd]	傷				1097
divorce [divɔ́ːrs]	離婚				1098
tune [tjúːn]	曲				1099
height [háit]	高さ				1100

3

Essential

No.	英語フレーズ	フレーズ書きこみ	日本語フレーズ
1101	the science faculty		理学部
1102	the average *life* span		平均寿命
1103	the moral dimension of science		科学の道徳的側面
1104	the latest version of the software		そのソフトの最新版
1105	have no parallel in history		歴史上匹敵するものがない
1106	the moon rising <u>on</u> the horizon		地平線に昇る月
1107	friends and acquaintances		友人と知人
1108	become a burden <u>on</u> society		社会の重荷になる
1109	the scientific basis of his theory		彼の理論の科学的根拠
1110	poison gas		毒ガス
1111	the Constitution of Japan		日本国憲法
1112	business administration		企業の経営
1113	a city full of charm		魅力にあふれた都市
1114	sense organs		感覚器官
1115	the prey of the lion		ライオンのえじき
1116	a *joint* venture with Taiwan		台湾との共同事業
1117	carry out a dangerous mission		危険な任務を果たす
1118	an inquiry into the accident		事故に関する調査
1119	the Academy Award *for* Best Picture		アカデミー最優秀作品賞
1120	a long strip of paper		長い紙切れ
1121	be in economic distress		経済的苦難におちいる
1122	increase blood circulation		血液の循環を高める
1123	keep the beer in the shade		ビールを日陰に置く
1124	a stereotype of Americans		アメリカ人に関する型にはまったイメージ
1125	a lawyer and his client		弁護士とその依頼人
1126	the factory's output		その工場の生産高
1127	praise the Lord		神をたたえる
1128	follow social conventions		社会の慣習に従う
1129	discover a gold mine		金鉱を発見する
1130	a traditional Japanese craft		日本の伝統工芸

単語	意味	書きこみ①	書きこみ②	書きこみ③	No.
faculty [fǽkəlti]	学部				1101
span [spǽn]	期間				1102
dimension [dimén∫ən]	側面				1103
version [vɔ́ːrʒən]	型				1104
parallel [pǽrəlel]	類似（物）				1105
horizon [həráizn]	地平線				1106
acquaintance [əkwéintəns]	知人				1107
burden [bɔ́ːrdn]	重荷				1108
basis [béisis]	基礎				1109
poison [pɔ́izn]	毒				1110
constitution [kɑnstətjúː∫ən]	憲法				1111
administration [ədministréi∫ən]	経営				1112
charm [t∫áːrm]	魅力				1113
organ [ɔ́ːrgən]	臓器				1114
prey [préi]	獲物				1115
venture [vént∫ər]	冒険的事業				1116
mission [mí∫ən]	使命				1117
inquiry [inkwáiəri]	調査				1118
award [əwɔ́ːrd]	賞				1119
strip [stríp]	細長い一片				1120
distress [distrés]	苦しみ				1121
circulation [səːrkjuléi∫ən]	循環				1122
shade [∫éid]	陰				1123
stereotype [stériətaip]	典型的なイメージ				1124
client [kláiənt]	依頼人				1125
output [áutput]	生産高				1126
lord [lɔ́ːrd]	神				1127
convention [kənvén∫ən]	慣習				1128
mine [máin]	鉱山				1129
craft [krǽft]	工芸				1130

3 Essential

No.	英語フレーズ	フレーズ書きこみ	日本語フレーズ
1131	the core *of* the problem		問題の核心
1132	have a stroke		脳卒中になる
1133	America's last frontier		アメリカ最後の辺境
1134	He's popular with his peers.		彼は同僚に人気だ
1135	blood vessels		血管
1136	people with disabilities		障害を持つ人々
1137	zero gravity in space		宇宙の無重力状態
1138	a question of medical ethics		医学の倫理の問題
1139	a railroad terminal		鉄道の終点
1140	swim against the tide		潮流に逆らって泳ぐ
1141	child abuse		児童虐待
1142	feel guilty about leaving him		彼を捨てたことに罪の意識を感じる
1143	be vital *to* human health		人の健康にきわめて重要だ
1144	his fellow workers		彼の仕事仲間
1145	contemporary Japanese society		現代の日本社会
1146	his annual income		彼の年収
1147	become accustomed *to* driv*ing*		車の運転に慣れる
1148	steady economic growth		着実な経済成長
1149	very dull work		とても退屈な仕事
1150	I'm keen *to* talk to him.		私は彼と話をしたい
1151	wear loose clothes		ゆったりとした服を着る
1152	the delicate balance of nature		自然界の微妙なバランス
1153	internal medicine		内科
1154	wear casual clothes		気楽な服装をする
1155	mature adults		成熟した大人
1156	give a concrete example		具体的な例をあげる
1157	How awful!		なんてひどい!
1158	be exhausted from overwork		過労で疲れ切っている
1159	part of an overall plan		全体的な計画の一部
1160	tight jeans		きついジーンズ

単語	意味	書きこみ①	書きこみ②	書きこみ③	No.
core [kɔ́ːr]	中心				1131
stroke [stróuk]	脳卒中				1132
frontier [frʌntíər]	国境				1133
peer [píər]	同僚				1134
vessel [vésl]	血管				1135
disability [dìsəbíləti]	障害				1136
gravity [grǽvəti]	重力				1137
ethic [éθik]	倫理(学)				1138
terminal [tɔ́ːrmənl]	終点				1139
tide [táid]	潮流				1140
abuse [əbjúːs] 動[əbjúːz]	虐待				1141
guilty [gílti]	有罪の				1142
vital [váitl]	きわめて重要な				1143
fellow [félou]	仲間の				1144
contemporary [kəntémpəreri]	現代の				1145
annual [ǽnjuəl]	年に1度の				1146
accustomed [əkʌ́stəmd]	慣れた				1147
steady [stédi]	しっかりした				1148
dull [dʌ́l]	退屈させる				1149
keen [kíːn]	熱望して				1150
loose [lúːs]	ゆるい				1151
delicate [délikət]	繊細な				1152
internal [intɔ́ːrnəl]	内部の				1153
casual [kǽʒuəl]	形式ばらない				1154
mature [mətúər]	成熟した				1155
concrete [kánkriːt]	具体的な				1156
awful [ɔ́ːfl]	ひどい				1157
exhausted [igzɔ́ːstid]	疲れ切っている				1158
overall [óuvərɔːl]	全面的な				1159
tight [táit]	引き締まった				1160

3

Essential

No.	英語フレーズ	フレーズ書きこみ	日本語フレーズ
1161 ☐	the prime cause		主要な原因
1162 ☐	a genuine interest in science		科学に対する真の関心
1163 ☐	a modest dress		控えめな服装
1164 ☐	an intimate relationship		親密な関係
1165 ☐	minimum effort		最小の努力
1166 ☐	sophisticated computer technology		高度なコンピュータ技術
1167 ☐	I have a dog and a cat. *The* latter is bigger.		犬と猫を飼っているが，後者の方が大きい
1168 ☐	a bitter experience		苦い経験
1169 ☐	expressions peculiar *to* English		英語特有の表現
1170 ☐	a passive attitude		消極的な態度
1171 ☐	different ethnic groups		異なる民族集団
1172 ☐	a person of noble birth		高貴な生まれの人
1173 ☐	make a vain effort		むだな努力をする
1174 ☐	blame innocent people		罪の無い人々を責める
1175 ☐	the underlying cause		根本的な原因
1176 ☐	an alien species		外来種
1177 ☐	be relevant *to* the question		その問題に関係がある
1178 ☐	I *am* inclined *to* believe him.		彼の言葉を信じたい気がする
1179 ☐	an awkward silence		気まずい沈黙
1180 ☐	That's a brilliant idea!		それはすばらしいアイディアだ!
1181 ☐	a desperate attempt		必死の試み
1182 ☐	a refreshing drink		さわやかな飲み物
1183 ☐	I'm thrilled to hear your voice.		君の声が聞けてとてもうれしい
1184 ☐	her inner self		彼女の内なる自分
1185 ☐	be consistent *with* the theory		理論と一致する
1186 ☐	be written in plain English		平易な英語で書かれている
1187 ☐	have vivid memories		鮮やかな思い出がある
1188 ☐	a miserable life		惨めな生活
1189 ☐	a substantial number of people		相当な数の人々
1190 ☐	She is very fond *of* reading.		彼女は読書が大好きだ

単語	意味	書きこみ①	書きこみ②	書きこみ③	No.
prime [práim]	最も重要な				1161
genuine [dʒénjuin]	本物の				1162
modest [mάdəst]	控えめな				1163
intimate [íntəmət]	親密な				1164
minimum [míniməm]	最小限の				1165
sophisticated [səfístikeitid]	高度な				1166
latter [lǽtər]	後者の				1167
bitter [bítər]	苦い				1168
peculiar [pikjúːliər]	独特の				1169
passive [pǽsiv]	受動的な				1170
ethnic [éθnik]	民族的な				1171
noble [nóubl]	高貴な				1172
vain [véin]	むだな				1173
innocent [ínəsənt]	無罪の				1174
underlying [ʌndərláiiŋ]	根本的な				1175
alien [éiljən]	外国（人）の				1176
relevant [réləvənt]	関連のある				1177
be inclined to V [inkláind]	Ｖしたい気がする				1178
awkward [ɔ́ːkwərd]	気まずい				1179
brilliant [bríljənt]	すばらしい				1180
desperate [déspərət]	必死の				1181
refreshing [rifréʃiŋ]	さわやかな				1182
thrilled [θríld]	とてもうれしい				1183
inner [ínər]	内側の				1184
consistent [kənsístənt]	矛盾のない				1185
plain [pléin]	明白な				1186
vivid [vívid]	鮮やかな				1187
miserable [mízərəbl]	惨めな				1188
substantial [səbstǽnʃəl]	相当な				1189
be fond of A [fάnd]	Ａが好きだ				1190

3

Essential

No.	英語フレーズ	フレーズ書きこみ	日本語フレーズ
1191	True or false?		正しいかまちがいか
1192	a lazy student		怠惰な学生
1193	precisely at noon		ちょうど正午に
1194	She was cooking. Meanwhile, I was drinking.		彼女は料理をしていた。その間, 私は酒を飲んでいた。
1195	disappear altogether		完全に消滅する
1196	Have you seen him lately?		最近彼に会いましたか
1197	barely survive the war		かろうじて戦争を生き延びる
1198	I could scarcely believe it.		ほとんど信じられなかった
1199	You're an adult, so act accordingly.		君は大人なのだからそれ相応に行動しなさい
1200	deliberately ignore him		彼をわざと無視する
1201	beneath the surface of the water		水面下で
1202	The British say "lift," whereas Americans say "elevator."		イギリス人は「リフト」と言うが, アメリカ人は「エレベータ」と言う
1203	declare independence from Britain		イギリスからの独立を宣言する
1204	alter the pattern of behavior		行動パターンを変える
1205	Problems arise *from* carelessness.		不注意から問題が生じる
1206	transform food *into* energy		食べ物をエネルギーに変える
1207	defeat the champion		チャンピオンを打ち負かす
1208	investigate the cause of the failure		失敗の原因を調査する
1209	distinguish a lie *from* the truth		うそと真実を見分ける
1210	bury treasure		宝物を埋める
1211	cope *with* problems		問題にうまく対処する
1212	This problem often occurs.		この問題はしばしば起こる
1213	accomplish the difficult task		困難な仕事をやりとげる
1214	Don't hesitate *to* ask questions.		質問するのをためらうな
1215	endure great pain		ひどい苦痛に耐える
1216	conclude that he is OK		彼は大丈夫だと結論づける
1217	guarantee your success		君の成功を保証する
1218	dominate the world economy		世界経済を支配する
1219	confirm Darwin's theory		ダーウィンの理論を裏づける
1220	greet people with a smile		笑顔で人にあいさつする

単語	意味	書きこみ①	書きこみ②	書きこみ③	No.
false [fɔ́:ls]	まちがいの				1191
lazy [léizi]	怠惰な				1192
precisely [prisáisli]	正確に				1193
meanwhile [mí:nhwail]	その間に				1194
altogether [ɔ:ltəgéðər]	完全に				1195
lately [léitli]	最近				1196
barely [béərli]	かろうじて				1197
scarcely [skéərsli]	ほとんど～ない				1198
accordingly [əkɔ́:rdiŋli]	それ相応に				1199
deliberately [dilíbərətli]	わざと				1200
beneath [biní:θ]	前 ～の下で				1201
whereas [hweəræz]	接 ～だが一方				1202
declare [dikléər]	～を宣言する				1203
alter [ɔ́:ltər]	～を変える				1204
arise [əráiz]	生じる				1205
transform [trænsfɔ́:rm]	変える				1206
defeat [difí:t]	～を打ち負かす				1207
investigate [invéstəgeit]	～を調査する				1208
distinguish [distíŋwiʃ]	～を見分ける				1209
bury [béri]	～を埋める				1210
cope [kóup]	うまく対処する				1211
occur [əkɔ́:r]	起こる				1212
accomplish [əkámpliʃ]	～をやりとげる				1213
hesitate [héziteit]	ためらう				1214
endure [endʲúər]	～に耐える				1215
conclude [kənklú:d]	結論づける				1216
guarantee [gærəntí:]	～を保証する				1217
dominate [dáməneit]	～を支配する				1218
confirm [kənfɔ́:rm]	～を裏づける				1219
greet [grí:t]	～にあいさつする				1220

3
Essential

No.	英語フレーズ	フレーズ書きこみ	日本語フレーズ
1221	entertain the audience		観客を楽しませる
1222	defend ourselves *against* attack		攻撃から自分たちを守る
1223	forbid him *to* go out		彼の外出を禁じる
1224	broadcast the concert live		生でコンサートを放送する
1225	sacrifice everything for love		愛のためすべてを犠牲にする
1226	punish him *for* the crime		その罪で彼を罰する
1227	glance *at* the clock		時計をちらりと見る
1228	retain the world title		世界タイトルを保持する
1229	calculate the cost		コストを計算する
1230	leave a sinking ship		沈む船から逃げる
1231	rescue a man from a fire		火事で人を救助する
1232	beg him *to* come back		彼に帰って来てと乞う
1233	define a day *as* twenty-four hours		1日を24時間と定義する
1234	It is easy to deceive people.		人をだますのは簡単だ
1235	convey information		情報を伝える
1236	energy to sustain life		生命を維持するためのエネルギー
1237	purchase the land		その土地を購入する
1238	Memories of the war fade *away*.		戦争の記憶が薄れる
1239	regulate traffic		交通を規制する
1240	distribute food equally		平等に食料を分配する
1241	enhance the quality of life		生活の質を向上させる
1242	chat *with* friends		友達とおしゃべりする
1243	Demand exceeds supply.		需要が供給を超える
1244	wipe the table		テーブルをふく
1245	cooperate *with* each other		お互いに協力する
1246	inherit genes *from* our parents		親から遺伝子を受け継ぐ
1247	unite the Arab world		アラブ世界を団結させる
1248	Look before you leap.		跳ぶ前によく見よ
1249	exaggerate the size of the fish		魚の大きさを誇張する
1250	conquer the world		世界を征服する

単語	意味	書きこみ①	書きこみ②	書きこみ③	No.
entertain [èntərtéin]	～を楽しませる				1221
defend [difénd]	～を守る				1222
forbid [fərbíd]	～を禁じる				1223
broadcast [brɔ́:dkæst]	～を放送する				1224
sacrifice [sǽkrəfais]	～を犠牲にする				1225
punish [pʌ́niʃ]	～を罰する				1226
glance [glǽns]	ちらりと見る				1227
retain [ritéin]	～を保持する				1228
calculate [kǽlkjəleit]	～を計算する				1229
sink [síŋk]	沈む				1230
rescue [réskju:]	～を救助する				1231
beg [bég]	～と乞う				1232
define [difáin]	定義する				1233
deceive [disí:v]	～をだます				1234
convey [kənvéi]	～を伝える				1235
sustain [səstéin]	～を維持する				1236
purchase [pə́:rtʃəs]	～を購入する				1237
fade [féid]	薄れる				1238
regulate [régjəleit]	～を規制する				1239
distribute [distríbju:t]	～を分配する				1240
enhance [inhǽns]	～を向上させる				1241
chat [tʃǽt]	おしゃべりする				1242
exceed [iksí:d]	～を超える				1243
wipe [wáip]	～をふく				1244
cooperate [kouápəreit]	協力する				1245
inherit [inhérit]	～を受け継ぐ				1246
unite [ju:náit]	～を団結させる				1247
leap [lí:p]	跳ぶ				1248
exaggerate [igzǽdʒəreit]	～を誇張する				1249
conquer [káŋkər]	～を征服する				1250

3

Essential

No.	英語フレーズ	フレーズ書きこみ	日本語フレーズ
1251	The snow will melt soon.		雪は間もなく溶けるだろう
1252	invade Poland		ポーランドに侵入する
1253	modify the plan		計画を修正する
1254	scatter toys on the floor		床におもちゃをばらまく
1255	undergo great changes		大きな変化を経験する
1256	evaluate online information		オンライン情報を評価する
1257	bend down to pick up the can		カンを拾おうと身をかがめる
1258	The word derives *from* Latin.		その単語はラテン語に由来する
1259	a girl screaming for help		助けを求め悲鳴をあげる少女
1260	gaze *at* the stars		星を見つめる
1261	pray for a sick child		病気の子供のために祈る
1262	polish the shoes		靴を磨く
1263	classify man *as* an animal		人間を動物として分類する
1264	assert *that* it is impossible		それは不可能だと主張する
1265	grab him by the arm		彼の腕をつかむ
1266	fold a piece of paper		紙を折りたたむ
1267	sweep the floor		床を掃く
1268	whisper in her ear		彼女の耳にささやく
1269	imitate human behavior		人間の行動をまねる
1270	stop and stare *at* her		立ち止まって彼女をじっと見る
1271	emphasize the importance of health		健康の大切さを強調する
1272	*get* rid *of* stress		ストレスを取り除く
1273	pour wine into the glass		グラスにワインを注ぐ
1274	vanish from sight		視界から消える
1275	restore the old building		古い建物を修復する
1276	deserve *to be* punished		罰を受けて当然だ
1277	a space science laboratory		宇宙科学研究所
1278	an international conference		国際会議
1279	cross the American continent		アメリカ大陸を横断する
1280	national health insurance		国民健康保険

単語	意味	書きこみ①	書きこみ②	書きこみ③	No.
melt [mélt]	溶ける				1251
invade [invéid]	〜に侵入する				1252
modify [mádifai]	〜を修正する				1253
scatter [skǽtər]	〜をばらまく				1254
undergo [ʌndərgóu]	〜を経験する				1255
evaluate [ivǽljueit]	〜を評価する				1256
bend [bénd]	身をかがめる				1257
derive [diráiv]	由来する				1258
scream [skríːm]	悲鳴をあげる				1259
gaze [géiz]	見つめる				1260
pray [préi]	祈る				1261
polish [páliʃ]	〜を磨く				1262
classify [klǽsifai]	分類する				1263
assert [əsə́ːrt]	〜と主張する				1264
grab [grǽb]	〜をつかむ				1265
fold [fóuld]	〜を折りたたむ				1266
sweep [swíːp]	〜を掃く				1267
whisper [hwíspər]	ささやく				1268
imitate [íməteit]	〜をまねる				1269
stare [stéər]	じっと見る				1270
emphasize [émfəsaiz]	〜を強調する				1271
rid [ríd]	〜を取り除く				1272
pour [pɔ́ːr]	〜を注ぐ				1273
vanish [vǽniʃ]	消える				1274
restore [ristɔ́ːr]	〜を修復する				1275
deserve [dizə́ːrv]	当然だ				1276
laboratory [lǽbərətɔːri]	研究所				1277
conference [kánfərəns]	会議				1278
continent [kántinənt]	大陸				1279
insurance [inʃúərəns]	保険				1280

3 Essential

No.	英語フレーズ	フレーズ書きこみ	日本語フレーズ
1281	the crew of the space shuttle		スペースシャトルの乗組員たち
1282	live in poverty		貧乏な生活をする
1283	water shortage		水不足
1284	international affairs		国際情勢
1285	the only exception *to* the rule		その規則の唯一の例外
1286	work for *low* wages		安い賃金で働く
1287	knowledge and wisdom		知識と知恵
1288	pay taxes *on* the land		その土地にかかる税金を払う
1289	human evolution		人類の進化
1290	the language barrier		言葉の壁
1291	fall into the same category		同じ範ちゅうに属する
1292	the family as a social unit		社会の単位としての家族
1293	the restaurant's reputation		そのレストランの評判
1294	the virtue of hard work		勤勉の美徳
1295	have the courage *to* tell the truth		真実を話す勇気を持つ
1296	feel sympathy *for* the victim		犠牲者に同情する
1297	a labor union		労働組合
1298	Western civilization		西洋文明
1299	a 10,000-volume library		蔵書1万冊の図書館
1300	cherry blossoms		サクラの花
1301	the beginning of a new era		新しい時代の始まり
1302	*settle* international disputes		国際紛争を解決する
1303	the tourism industry in Japan		日本の観光産業
1304	the history of mankind		人類の歴史
1305	mass murder		大量殺人
1306	landscape painting		風景画
1307	reach the final destination		最終目的地に着く
1308	tell a *fairy* tale		おとぎ話をする
1309	political reform		政治改革
1310	muscles and bones		筋肉と骨

単語	意味	書きこみ①	書きこみ②	書きこみ③	No.
crew [krúː]	乗組員たち				1281
poverty [pávərti]	貧乏				1282
shortage [ʃɔ́ːrtidʒ]	不足				1283
affair [əféər]	情勢				1284
exception [iksépʃən]	例外				1285
wage [wéidʒ]	賃金				1286
wisdom [wízdəm]	知恵				1287
tax [tǽks]	税金				1288
evolution [evəljúːʃən]	進化				1289
barrier [bǽriər]	壁				1290
category [kǽtəgɔːri]	範ちゅう				1291
unit [júːnit]	単位				1292
reputation [repjutéiʃən]	評判				1293
virtue [vɔ́ːrtʃuː]	美徳				1294
courage [kɔ́ːridʒ]	勇気				1295
sympathy [símpəθi]	同情				1296
union [júːnjən]	組合				1297
civilization [sivəlizéiʃən]	文明				1298
volume [válju(ː)m]	冊				1299
blossom [blásəm]	花				1300
era [íːrə]	時代				1301
dispute [dispjúːt]	紛争				1302
tourism [túərizm]	観光				1303
mankind [mǽnkáind]	人類				1304
murder [mɔ́ːrdər]	殺人				1305
landscape [lǽndskeip]	風景				1306
destination [destinéiʃən]	目的地				1307
tale [téil]	話				1308
reform [rifɔ́ːrm]	改革				1309
muscle [mʌ́sl]	筋肉				1310

3

Essential

No.	英語フレーズ	フレーズ書きこみ	日本語フレーズ
1311 ☐	future prospects		将来の見通し
1312 ☐	run a large corporation		大企業を経営する
1313 ☐	a former British colony		元イギリスの植民地
1314 ☐	a quarrel *with* my wife		妻との口論
1315 ☐	an intellectual profession		知的職業
1316 ☐	unique aspects *of* Japanese culture		日本文化のユニークな側面
1317 ☐	a three-minute pause		3分間の休止
1318 ☐	the conflict *between* the two sides		その両者間の対立
1319 ☐	white privilege		白人の特権
1320 ☐	economic prosperity		経済的繁栄
1321 ☐	a musical genius		音楽の天才
1322 ☐	plant pumpkin seeds		カボチャの種をまく
1323 ☐	symptoms of a cold		カゼの症状
1324 ☐	his greatest merit		彼の最大の長所
1325 ☐	destroy the ozone layer		オゾン層を破壊する
1326 ☐	a clue *to* the mystery		その謎を解く手がかり
1327 ☐	*under* any circumstances		いかなる状況においても
1328 ☐	the city's business district		その都市の商業地区
1329 ☐	spend two years in prison		刑務所で2年過ごす
1330 ☐	my traveling companion		私の旅行仲間
1331 ☐	chief executive officer		最高経営責任者 (CEO)
1332 ☐	a strong sense of justice		強い正義感
1333 ☐	the check-in procedure		チェックインの手続き
1334 ☐	the sun's rays		太陽光線
1335 ☐	go to heaven		天国に昇る
1336 ☐	lead a life of luxury		ぜいたくな生活を送る
1337 ☐	oxygen in the air		空気中の酸素
1338 ☐	lack of funds		資金不足
1339 ☐	the theme of the book		その本の主題
1340 ☐	the boundary *between* two countries		二国間の境界

単語	意味	書きこみ①	書きこみ②	書きこみ③	No.
prospect [práspekt]	見通し				1311
corporation [kɔːrpəréiʃən]	企業				1312
colony [káləni]	植民地				1313
quarrel [kwɔ́(ː)rəl]	口論				1314
profession [prəféʃən]	職業				1315
aspect [ǽspekt]	側面				1316
pause [pɔ́ːz]	休止				1317
conflict [kánflikt]　動 [kənflíkt]	対立				1318
privilege [prívilidʒ]	特権				1319
prosperity [prɑspérəti]	繁栄				1320
genius [dʒíːnjəs]	天才				1321
seed [síːd]	種				1322
symptom [símptəm]	症状				1323
merit [mérit]	長所				1324
layer [léiər]	層				1325
clue [klúː]	手がかり				1326
circumstances [sɔ́ːrkəmstænsiz]	状況				1327
district [dístrikt]	地区				1328
prison [prízn]	刑務所				1329
companion [kəmpǽnjən]	仲間				1330
executive [igzékjətiv]	経営責任者				1331
justice [dʒʌ́stis]	正義				1332
procedure [prəsíːdʒər]	手続き				1333
ray [réi]	光線				1334
heaven [hévən]	天国				1335
luxury [lʌ́gʒəri]	ぜいたく				1336
oxygen [ɑ́ksidʒən]	酸素				1337
fund [fʌ́nd]	資金				1338
theme [θíːm]	主題				1339
boundary [báundəri]	境界				1340

3

Essential

No.	英語フレーズ	フレーズ書きこみ	日本語フレーズ
1341	his ambition *to* be a writer		作家になりたいという彼の熱望
1342	the *weather* forecast		天気予報
1343	study social psychology		社会心理学を研究する
1344	do hard labor		重労働を行う
1345	the International Olympic Committee		国際オリンピック委員会 (IOC)
1346	a physician at the hospital		その病院の医者
1347	his philosophy of life		彼の人生哲学
1348	a deep affection *for* animals		動物への深い愛情
1349	a candidate *for* President		大統領候補
1350	an atomic bomb		原子爆弾
1351	give top priority to safety		安全を最優先する
1352	an obstacle *to* communication		コミュニケーションの障害
1353	have no appetite		食欲がない
1354	relieve tension		緊張を緩和する
1355	a Native American tribe		アメリカ先住民の部族
1356	cut the defense budget		防衛予算を削減する
1357	the campaign *to* promote tourism		観光を促進する運動
1358	joy and sorrow		喜びと悲しみ
1359	a communications satellite		通信衛星
1360	a deep insight *into* life		人生に対する深い洞察
1361	have a bad cough		ひどいせきが出る
1362	decide the fate of the world		世界の運命を決定する
1363	a training scheme for pilots		パイロットの訓練計画
1364	an insult to women		女性に対する侮辱
1365	the inhabitants *of* the country		その国の住民
1366	burn fossil *fuels*		化石燃料を燃やす
1367	the motive for the crime		犯罪の動機
1368	human instinct to fight		人間の闘争本能
1369	the legend of Robin Hood		ロビン・フッドの伝説
1370	the Roman Empire		ローマ帝国

⑹名詞：本冊 p. 281 〜 285

単語	意味	書きこみ①	書きこみ②	書きこみ③	No.
ambition [æmbíʃən]	熱望				1341
forecast [fɔ́ːrkæst]	予報				1342
psychology [saikálədʒi]	心理学				1343
labor [léibər]	労働				1344
committee [kəmíti:]	委員会				1345
physician [fizíʃən]	医者				1346
philosophy [filásəfi]	哲学				1347
affection [əfékʃən]	愛情				1348
candidate [kǽndideit]	候補				1349
bomb [bám]	爆弾				1350
priority [praió(:)rəti]	優先				1351
obstacle [ábstəkl]	障害				1352
appetite [ǽpitait]	食欲				1353
tension [ténʃən]	緊張				1354
tribe [tráib]	部族				1355
budget [bʌ́dʒit]	予算				1356
campaign [kæmpéin]	運動				1357
sorrow [sárou]	悲しみ				1358
satellite [sǽtəlait]	衛星				1359
insight [ínsait]	洞察				1360
cough [kɔ́(:)f]	せき				1361
fate [féit]	運命				1362
scheme [skíːm]	計画				1363
insult [ínsʌlt] 🔊 [insʌ́lt]	侮辱				1364
inhabitant [inhǽbitənt]	住民				1365
fossil [fá(:)səl]	化石				1366
motive [móutiv]	動機				1367
instinct [ínstiŋkt]	本能				1368
legend [lédʒənd]	伝説				1369
empire [émpaiər]	帝国				1370

3

Essential

No.	英語フレーズ	フレーズ書きこみ	日本語フレーズ
1371	live in the suburbs of London		ロンドンの郊外に住む
1372	study modern architecture		近代建築を学ぶ
1373	love and passion		愛と情熱
1374	the treatment of cancer		がんの治療
1375	persuade him with logic		彼を論理で説得する
1376	two dozen eggs		2ダースの卵
1377	a good harvest of rice		米の豊かな収穫
1378	the ingredients of the cake		ケーキの材料
1379	*test* the hypothesis		仮説を検証する
1380	the first voyage of Columbus		コロンブスの最初の航海
1381	the editor of a fashion magazine		ファッション雑誌の編集長
1382	have no option		選択の自由がない
1383	the southern hemisphere		南半球
1384	the mechanism of a clock		時計の仕組み
1385	Anthropologists study people.		人類学者は人間を研究する
1386	Greek tragedy		ギリシャ悲劇
1387	resistance to antibiotics		抗生物質に対する耐性
1388	pay the bus fare		バスの運賃を払う
1389	pay the debt		借金を返す
1390	the high school curriculum		高校の教育課程
1391	the components of the body		人体の構成要素
1392	plant wheat and corn		小麦とコーンを植える
1393	modern English usage		現代英語の語法
1394	a sand castle		砂の城
1395	a terrible famine in Africa		アフリカのひどい飢饉（ききん）
1396	animals in danger of extinction		絶滅の危機にある動物たち
1397	take money out of the purse		財布からお金を取り出す
1398	English folk music		イギリスの民族音楽
1399	the population explosion		人口爆発
1400	*a* large portion *of* your salary		給料の大部分

単語	意味	書きこみ①	書きこみ②	書きこみ③	No.
suburb [sʌ́bəːrb]	郊外				1371
architecture [ɑ́ːrkitektʃər]	建築				1372
passion [pǽʃən]	情熱				1373
cancer [kǽnsər]	がん				1374
logic [ládʒik]	論理				1375
dozen [dʌ́zn]	ダース				1376
harvest [háːrvist]	収穫				1377
ingredient [ingríːdiənt]	材料				1378
hypothesis [haipáθəsis]	仮説				1379
voyage [vɔ́iidʒ]	航海				1380
editor [éditər]	編集長				1381
option [ápʃən]	選択の自由				1382
hemisphere [hémisfiər]	半球				1383
mechanism [mékənizm]	仕組み				1384
anthropologist [ænθrəpálədʒist]	人類学者				1385
tragedy [trǽdʒədi]	悲劇				1386
antibiotic [æntibaiátik]	抗生物質				1387
fare [féər]	運賃				1388
debt [dét]	借金				1389
curriculum [kəríkjələm]	教育課程				1390
component [kəmpóunənt]	構成要素				1391
wheat [ʰwiːt]	小麦				1392
usage [júːsidʒ]	語法				1393
castle [kǽsl]	城				1394
famine [fǽmin]	飢饉				1395
extinction [ikstíŋkʃən]	絶滅				1396
purse [pə́ːrs]	財布				1397
folk [fóuk]	民族				1398
explosion [iksplóuʒən]	爆発				1399
portion [pɔ́ːrʃən]	部分				1400

3 Essential

No.	英語フレーズ	フレーズ書きこみ	日本語フレーズ
1401	marine organisms		海洋生物
1402	The Merchant of Venice		ヴェニスの商人
1403	ancient Greek myths		古代ギリシャの神話
1404	the small incidents of everyday life		日常生活の小さな出来事
1405	protect wildlife		野生生物を保護する
1406	the United States Congress		合衆国議会
1407	a boat in Tokyo Bay		東京湾に浮かぶ船
1408	the death penalty		死刑
1409	Japanese cultural heritage		日本の文化遺産
1410	American cultural diversity		アメリカの文化的多様性
1411	the thumb of my left hand		私の左手の親指
1412	history and geography		歴史と地理
1413	an important factor _in_ success		成功の重要な要因
1414	discrimination _against_ women		女性に対する差別
1415	the flu virus		インフルエンザウイルス
1416	the Statue of Liberty		自由の女神像
1417	a priest in the church		教会の神父
1418	a rock'n'roll pioneer		ロックンロールの先駆者
1419	personality traits		人格の特徴
1420	strong family bonds		家族の強いきずな
1421	go to the grocery store		食料品店に行く
1422	his secretary's desk		彼の秘書の机
1423	speak the local dialect		地元の方言を話す
1424	Galileo's astronomy		ガリレオの天文学
1425	today's youngsters		今日の子供たち
1426	a dangerous substance		危険な物質
1427	recent research findings		最近の研究による発見
1428	British military strategy		イギリスの軍事戦略
1429	his heart and lungs		彼の心臓と肺
1430	beat an opponent		敵を倒す

単語	意味	書きこみ①	書きこみ②	書きこみ③	No.
organism [ɔ́ːrgænizm]	生物				1401
merchant [mɔ́ːrtʃənt]	商人				1402
myth [míθ]	神話				1403
incident [ínsidənt]	出来事				1404
wildlife [wáildlaif]	野生生物				1405
congress [káŋgrəs]	議会				1406
bay [béi]	湾				1407
penalty [pénəlti]	刑				1408
heritage [héritidʒ]	遺産				1409
diversity [divɔ́ːrsəti]	多様性				1410
thumb [θʌ́m]	親指				1411
geography [dʒiágrəfi]	地理				1412
factor [fǽktər]	要因				1413
discrimination [diskriminéiʃən]	差別				1414
virus [váiərəs]	ウイルス				1415
statue [stǽtʃuː]	像				1416
priest [príːst]	神父				1417
pioneer [paiəníər]	先駆者				1418
trait [tréit]	特徴				1419
bond [bánd]	きずな				1420
grocery [gróusəri]	食料品				1421
secretary [sékrəteri]	秘書				1422
dialect [dáiəlckt]	方言				1423
astronomy [əstránəmi]	天文学				1424
youngster [jʌ́ŋstər]	子供				1425
substance [sʌ́bstəns]	物質				1426
finding [fáindiŋ]	発見				1427
strategy [strǽtədʒi]	戦略				1428
lung [lʌ́ŋ]	肺				1429
opponent [əpóunənt]	敵				1430

3

Essential

No.	英語フレーズ	フレーズ書きこみ	日本語フレーズ
1431	a religious ritual		宗教的な儀式
1432	the outcome of the race		レースの結果
1433	conservation groups		環境保護団体
1434	whales and other sea mammals		クジラなどの海の哺乳類
1435	NASA's space telescope		NASAの宇宙望遠鏡
1436	refugee camps in Palestine		パレスチナの難民キャンプ
1437	a strict dress code		厳しい服装規則
1438	the flavor of fresh fruit		新鮮なフルーツの風味
1439	the particles of light		光の粒子
1440	24-hour nursing		24時間看護
1441	commit suicide		自殺をする
1442	the natural habitat of bears		クマの自然生息地
1443	bullying in schools		学校のいじめ
1444	Dinosaurs died out.		恐竜は絶滅した
1445	the New York City Council		ニューヨーク市議会
1446	age and gender		年齢と性別
1447	have open heart surgery		心臓切開手術を受ける
1448	technological innovation		技術革新
1449	high-protein food		高タンパク質の食べ物
1450	enough sleep and nutrition		十分な睡眠と栄養
1451	prepare for *natural* disaster		自然災害に備える
1452	greenhouse gas emissions		温室効果ガスの排出
1453	monkeys and apes		猿と類人猿
1454	a single DNA molecule		1つのDNA分子
1455	the smell of sweat		汗の臭い
1456	a heart transplant operation		心臓移植の手術
1457	many species of birds		多くの種の鳥
1458	the tip of my finger		私の指の先
1459	raise sheep and cattle		羊と牛を育てる
1460	high population density		高い人口密度

単語	意味	書きこみ①	書きこみ②	書きこみ③	No.
ritual [rítʃuəl]	儀式				1431
outcome [áutkʌm]	結果				1432
conservation [kɑnsərvéiʃən]	環境保護				1433
mammal [mǽməl]	哺乳類				1434
telescope [téləskoup]	望遠鏡				1435
refugee [refjudʒíː]	難民				1436
code [kóud]	規則				1437
flavor [fléivər]	風味				1438
particle [páːrtikl]	粒子				1439
nursing [nə́ːrsiŋ]	看護				1440
suicide [súːəsaid]	自殺				1441
habitat [hǽbitæt]	生息地				1442
bullying [búliiŋ]	いじめ				1443
dinosaur [dáinəsɔːr]	恐竜				1444
council [káunsl]	議会				1445
gender [dʒéndər]	性別				1446
surgery [sə́ːrdʒəri]	手術				1447
innovation [inəvéiʃən]	革新				1448
protein [próutiːn]	タンパク質				1449
nutrition [njuːtríʃən]	栄養				1450
disaster [dizǽstər]	災害				1451
emission [imíʃən]	排出				1452
ape [éip]	類人猿				1453
molecule [mάləkjuːl]	分子				1454
sweat [swét]	汗				1455
transplant [trǽnsplænt] 動 [— ´]	移植				1456
species [spíːʃiːz]	種				1457
tip [típ]	先				1458
cattle [kǽtl]	牛				1459
density [dénsəti]	密度				1460

3

Essential

No.	英語フレーズ	フレーズ書きこみ	日本語フレーズ
1461	the concept _of_ time		時間の概念
1462	You look pale.		君は青白い顔をしている
1463	precious jewels		貴重な宝石
1464	a worker loyal _to_ the company		会社に忠実な労働者
1465	be isolated _from_ the world		世界から孤立している
1466	a generous offer		気前のよい申し出
1467	tropical rain forests		熱帯雨林
1468	_be_ reluctant _to_ talk about the past		過去について話したがらない
1469	a vague feeling of uneasiness		漠然とした不安感
1470	the vast land of Russia		ロシアの広大な土地
1471	numerous species of birds		たくさんの種の鳥
1472	move to a small rural town		小さな田舎の町に引っ越す
1473	the widespread use of cell phones		広まっている携帯電話の利用
1474	a complicated problem		複雑な問題
1475	make visible progress		目に見える進歩をとげる
1476	eat raw meat		生の肉を食べる
1477	live in a remote village		へんぴな村に住む
1478	need urgent action		緊急の行動を必要とする
1479	tell silly jokes		ばかな冗談を言う
1480	a striking contrast		いちじるしい対照
1481	provide adequate food		十分な食料を供給する
1482	a man of extraordinary talent		並はずれた才能の持ち主
1483	the odd couple		おかしな2人
1484	an abstract concept		抽象的な概念
1485	mutual understanding		相互の理解
1486	excessive use of alcohol		過度のアルコール摂取
1487	I'_m_ ashamed _of_ myself.		自分が恥ずかしい
1488	a tremendous amount of energy		とてつもない量のエネルギー
1489	Change is inevitable.		変化は避けられない
1490	pure gold		純金

単語	意味	書きこみ①	書きこみ②	書きこみ③	No.
concept [kánsept]	概念				1461
pale [péil]	青白い				1462
precious [préʃəs]	貴重な				1463
loyal [lɔ́iəl]	忠実な				1464
isolated [áisəleitid]	孤立している				1465
generous [dʒénərəs]	気前のよい				1466
tropical [trápikəl]	熱帯の				1467
reluctant [rilʌ́ktənt]	したがらない				1468
vague [véig]	漠然とした				1469
vast [vǽst]	広大な				1470
numerous [njúːmərəs]	たくさんの				1471
rural [rúərəl]	田舎の				1472
widespread [wáidspréd]	広まっている				1473
complicated [kámpləkeitəd]	複雑な				1474
visible [vízəbl]	目に見える				1475
raw [rɔ́ː]	生の				1476
remote [rimóut]	へんぴな				1477
urgent [ə́ːrdʒənt]	緊急の				1478
silly [síli]	ばかな				1479
striking [stráikiŋ]	いちじるしい				1480
adequate [ǽdikwət]	十分な				1481
extraordinary [ikstrɔ́ːrdəneri]	並はずれた				1482
odd [ád]	おかしな				1483
abstract [ǽbstrækt]	抽象的な				1484
mutual [mjúːtʃuəl]	相互の				1485
excessive [iksésiv]	過度の				1486
ashamed [əʃéimd]	恥ずかしい				1487
tremendous [triméndəs]	とてつもない				1488
inevitable [inévitəbl]	避けられない				1489
pure [pjúər]	純粋な				1490

3 Essential

No.	英語フレーズ	フレーズ書きこみ	日本語フレーズ
1491	a stable condition		安定した状態
1492	be indifferent *to* politics		政治に無関心だ
1493	children's aggressive behavior		子供の攻撃的な行動
1494	the ultimate goal		究極の目標
1495	a quiet, shy girl		静かで内気な女の子
1496	solar energy		太陽エネルギー
1497	a profound meaning		深い意味
1498	a subtle difference		微妙な違い
1499	the Conservative Party		保守党
1500	a brave young soldier		勇敢な若い兵士
1501	feel intense pressure		強烈なプレッシャーを感じる
1502	alcoholic drinks like wine		ワインのようなアルコール飲料
1503	manual work		手を使う仕事 (肉体労働)
1504	cruel treatment of animals		動物に対する残酷な扱い
1505	rational thought		理性的な思考
1506	the initial stages of development		発達の最初の段階
1507	the body's immune *system*		人体の免疫機構
1508	the linguistic ability of children		子供の言語能力
1509	play a crucial role		重大な役割を果たす
1510	verbal communication		言葉によるコミュニケーション
1511	an optimistic view of the future		将来に関する楽観的な見方
1512	have flexible thinking		柔軟な考えを持っている
1513	I'm grateful *for* your help.		君の助けに感謝している
1514	a lively conversation		生き生きとした会話
1515	an overwhelming majority		圧倒的な多数
1516	an abundant supply of food		豊富な食料供給
1517	a selfish attitude		利己的な態度
1518	an ugly duckling		みにくいアヒルの子
1519	racial differences		人種の違い
1520	a prominent scientist		有名な科学者

単語	意味	書きこみ①	書きこみ②	書きこみ③	No.
stable [stéibl]	安定した				1491
indifferent [indífərənt]	無関心な				1492
aggressive [əgrésiv]	攻撃的な				1493
ultimate [ʌ́ltimət]	究極の				1494
shy [ʃái]	内気な				1495
solar [sóulər]	太陽の				1496
profound [prəfáund]	深い				1497
subtle [sʌ́tl]	微妙な				1498
conservative [kənsə́:rvətiv]	保守の				1499
brave [bréiv]	勇敢な				1500
intense [inténs]	強烈な				1501
alcoholic [ælkəhɔ́lik]	アルコールの				1502
manual [mǽnjuəl]	手を使う				1503
cruel [krú:əl]	残酷な				1504
rational [rǽʃənəl]	理性的な				1505
initial [iníʃəl]	最初の				1506
immune [imjú:n]	免疫の				1507
linguistic [liŋgwístik]	言語の				1508
crucial [krú:ʃəl]	重大な				1509
verbal [və́:rbəl]	言葉による				1510
optimistic [ɑptimístik]	楽観的な				1511
flexible [fléksəbl]	柔軟な				1512
grateful [gréitfəl]	感謝している				1513
lively [láivli]	生き生きとした				1514
overwhelming [ouvərʰwélmiŋ]	圧倒的な				1515
abundant [əbʌ́ndənt]	豊富な				1516
selfish [sélfiʃ]	利己的な				1517
ugly [ʌ́gli]	みにくい				1518
racial [réiʃəl]	人種の				1519
prominent [prɑ́mənənt]	有名な				1520

3

Essential

No.	英語フレーズ	フレーズ書きこみ	日本語フレーズ
1521	a controversial social *issue*		物議を呼ぶ社会問題
1522	the Federal Government		連邦政府
1523	a ridiculous error		ばかげたまちがい
1524	an imaginary country		架空の国
	an imaginative writer		想像力豊かな作家
	every trouble imaginable		想像しうるあらゆる困難
1525	the harsh realities of life		厳しい人生の現実
1526	a random choice		無作為な選択
1527	adolescent boys and girls		思春期の少年少女
1528	up-to-date fashions		最新の流行
1529	liberal politics		自由主義の政治
1530	the period prior *to* the war		戦争より前の時代
1531	do moderate exercise		適度な運動をする
1532	be fluent *in* English		英語が流ちょうだ
1533	an elaborate system		手の込んだシステム
1534	an incredible story		信じられない話
1535	radical changes		根本的な変化
1536	acid rain		酸性雨
1537	sign language for deaf people		耳が不自由な人のための手話
1538	a medieval castle		中世の城
1539	protect the ecological system		生態系を保護する
1540	without the slightest doubt		少しの疑いもなく
1541	be ignorant *of* the fact		その事実を知らない
1542	children's cognitive abilities		子供の認知能力
1543	It's absolutely necessary.		絶対に必要だ
1544	virtually every woman		ほとんどすべての女性
1545	somewhat better than last year		去年より多少よい
1546	It is merely bad luck.		単に運が悪いだけです

単語	意味	書きこみ①	書きこみ②	書きこみ③	No.
controversial [kὰntrəvə́ːrʃəl]	物議を呼ぶ				1521
federal [fédərəl]	連邦の				1522
ridiculous [ridíkjuləs]	ばかげた				1523
imaginary [imǽdʒəneri]	架空の				1524
imaginative [imǽdʒənətiv]	想像力豊かな				
imaginable [imǽdʒənəbl]	想像しうる				
harsh [háːrʃ]	厳しい				1525
random [rǽndəm]	無作為な				1526
adolescent [æd̀əlésnt]	思春期の				1527
up-to-date [ʌ́ptədéit]	最新の				1528
liberal [líbərəl]	自由主義の				1529
prior [práiər]	前の				1530
moderate [mɑ́dərit]	適度な				1531
fluent [flúːənt]	流ちょうな				1532
elaborate [ilǽbərit]	手の込んだ				1533
incredible [inkrédəbl]	信じられない				1534
radical [rǽdikəl]	根本的な				1535
acid [ǽsid]	酸性の				1536
deaf [déf]	耳が不自由な				1537
medieval [mìːdíːvəl]	中世の				1538
ecological [èkəlɑ́dʒikəl]	生態の				1539
slight [sláit]	少しの				1540
ignorant [ígnərənt]	知らない				1541
cognitive [kɑ́gnətiv]	認知の				1542
absolutely [ǽbsəluːtli]	絶対に				1543
virtually [və́ːrtʃuəli]	ほとんど				1544
somewhat [sʌ́mhwɑt]	多少				1545
merely [míərli]	単に				1546

3 Essential

No.	英語フレーズ	フレーズ書きこみ	日本語フレーズ
1547 ☐	There's literally nothing there.		そこには文字通り何もない
☐	the literal meaning of the word		その単語の文字通りの意味
☐	literary history		文学の歴史
☐	literate people in India		読み書きのできるインド人
1548 ☐	a seemingly impossible task		一見不可能な仕事
1549 ☐	regardless _of_ age		年齢に関係なく
1550 ☐	thoroughly enjoy the party		パーティを徹底的に楽しむ

⑧副詞：本冊 p. 309 ～ 310

単語	意味	書きこみ①	書きこみ②	書きこみ③	No.
literally [lítərəli]	文字通りに				1547
literal [lítərəl]	文字通りの				
literary [lítərəri]	文学の				
literate [lítərət]	読み書きのできる				
seemingly [síːmiŋli]	一見				1548
regardless of A [rigáːrdləs]	Aに関係なく				1549
thoroughly [θɔ́ːrouli]	徹底的に				1550

3

Essential

Stage 4

多義語の Brush Up

"All's well that ends well."

* * *

終わりよければすべてよし。

No.	英語フレーズ	フレーズ書きこみ	日本語フレーズ
1	run a big company		動 大会社を経営する
2-1	meet people's needs		動 人々の必要を満たす
2-2	how to meet the problem		動 問題に対処する方法
3-1	the right to vote		名 投票する権利
3-2	right and wrong		名 善と悪
3-3	right in front of my house		副 私の家のすぐ前に
4-1	The war lasted four years.		動 戦争は4年続いた
4-2	Our food will last a week.		動 食料は一週間持つだろう
4-3	the last man who would tell a lie		形 最もうそをつきそうにない人
4-4	He's moved twice in *the* last year.		形 彼は最近1年間に2回引っ越した
5	I *can't* stand this heat.		動 この暑さには耐えられない
6-1	Now it's your turn.		名 さあ君の番だ
6-2	the turn of the century		名 世紀の変わり目
7-1	It is also *the* case *with* him.		名 それは彼についても事実だ
7-2	a murder case		名 殺人事件
7-3	make a case *for* war		名 戦争を支持する主張をする
7-4	new cases of malaria		名 マラリアの新しい患者
8-1	face a problem		動 問題に直面する
8-2	problems facing Japan		動 日本に迫っている問題
9-1	a certain amount of time		形 ある程度の時間
9-2	I am certain *of* his success.		形 私は彼の成功を確信している
9-3	He is certain to come.		形 彼が来るのは確実だ
10-1	keep bad company		名 悪い仲間とつきあう
10-2	I enjoy your company.		名 君と一緒にいることは楽しい
10-3	We have company today.		名 今日は来客がある
11-1	attend the meeting		動 ミーティングに出席する
11-2	attend to patients		動 患者を世話する
11-3	attend *to* what he says		動 彼の言うことに注意する

No.	英語フレーズ	フレーズ書きこみ	日本語フレーズ
12-1	He worked hard; otherwise he would have failed.		副 彼は努力した。さもなければ失敗しただろう。
12-2	He is poor but otherwise happy.		副 彼は貧しいがその他の点では幸福だ
12-3	He is honest, but people think otherwise.		副 彼は正直なのに人はちがうと思っている
12-4	I can't do it otherwise.		副 ちがう方法ではできない
13-1	miss the last train		動 終電車に乗り遅れる
13-2	I sometimes miss Japan.		動 時には日本が恋しい
13-3	You can't miss it.		動 見逃すはずないよ
14-1	use scientific terms		名 科学用語を使う
14-2	long-term planning		名 長期的な計画
14-3	I am *on* good terms *with* him.		名 彼とは仲がよい
15-1	theory and practice		名 理論と実践
15-2	business practice		名 商習慣
15-3	practice medicine		動 医者を営む
16-1	face a new challenge		名 新しい難問に直面する
16-2	challenge the theory		動 その理論に異議をとなえる
17	a race problem		名 人種問題
18-1	a political issue		名 政治問題
18-2	issue an order		動 命令を出す
18-3	the latest issue of *Time*		名 「タイム」の最新号
19-1	the Democratic Party		名 民主党
19-2	a party of tourists		名 観光客の一団
19-3	Your party is on the line.		名 相手の方が電話に出ています
20	There is no room for doubt.		名 疑問の余地はない
21-1	In a sense, it is right.		名 ある意味ではそれは正しい
21-2	He *came to his* senses.		名 彼は正気に戻った
22-1	This pen *will* do.		動 このペンで十分役に立つ
22-2	do harm *to* the area		動 その地域に害を与える
23-1	*play* a part *in* the economy		名 経済で役割を果たす
23-2	a fault *on* our part		名 私たちの側の過失
23-3	part *with* the car		動 車を手放す

4

多義語

No.	英語フレーズ	フレーズ書きこみ	日本語フレーズ
24-1 ☐	Tell me the exact figures.		名正確な数字を教えて くれ
24-2 ☐	historical figures		名歴史上の人物
24-3 ☐	She has a beautiful figure.		名彼女はスタイルが美 しい
24-4 ☐	I figure you are busy.		動君は忙しいと思う
25-1 ☐	his true character		名彼の本当の性格
25-2 ☐	He's an odd character.		名彼は変わった人物だ
25-3 ☐	the characters in the novel		名その小説の登場人物
26 ☐	*the* very man I was looking for		形私が探していたまさ にその男
27-1 ☐	order a book *from* England		動英国に本を注文する
27-2 ☐	carry out his order		名彼の命令を遂行する
27-3 ☐	law and order		名法と秩序
27-4 ☐	in alphabetical order		名アルファベット順で
28-1 ☐	That sounds true.		動それは本当らしく聞 こえる
28-2 ☐	a sound body		形健全な肉体
28-3 ☐	She is sound *asleep*.		副彼女はぐっすり眠って いる
29-1 ☐	*In* some ways they are right.		名いくつかの点で彼ら は正しい
29-2 ☐	The island is a long way off.		名その島までは距離が 遠い
29-3 ☐	Come this way, please.		名こちらの方へどうぞ
30-1 ☐	concern *about* the future		名将来への不安
30-2 ☐	concern *for* others		名他人への思いやり
30-3 ☐	This problem concerns everyone.		動この問題はみんなに 関係する
30-4 ☐	a matter *of* great concern		名大変重要な問題
31 ☐	This is even better.		副これはさらによい
32-1 ☐	He is still working.		副まだ彼は働いている
32-2 ☐	a still better idea		副さらによい考え
32-3 ☐	The water became still.		形水は静かになった
32-4 ☐	It's raining. Still, I have to go.		副雨だ。それでも行か ねばならない。
33-1 ☐	I meant *to* call you sooner.		動すぐに電話するつも りだった
33-2 ☐	I love you. I mean it.		動好きだ。本気で言っ てるんだ。
33-3 ☐	He is mean to me.		形彼は私に意地悪だ

No.	英語フレーズ	フレーズ書きこみ	日本語フレーズ
34-1	leave an umbrella on the train		動電車に傘を置き忘れる
34-2	leave the door open		動ドアを開けたまま放置する
34-3	There is little time left.		動残り時間はほとんどない
34-4	take paid parental leave		名有給の育児休暇を取る
35-1	Most people think so.		形たいていの人はそう考える
35-2	a most important point		副非常に重要な点
36	Things have changed.		名状況は変わった
37-1	against his will		名彼の意志に反して
37-2	leave a will		名遺言を残す
38-1	an excited state of mind		名興奮した精神状態
38-2	state an opinion		動意見を述べる
38-3	a state secret		名国家の機密
39-1	I *don't* mind walk*ing*.		動歩くのはいやではない
39-2	talented minds		名才能ある人々
40	I *cannot* help laugh*ing*.		動笑わずにはいられない
41-1	It *doesn't* matter what he says.		動彼が何と言おうと重要ではない
41-2	soft matter		名やわらかい物質
41-3	Something *is the* matter *with* my car.		名私の車はどこか異常だ
42-1	a means of communication		名コミュニケーションの手段
42-2	a man of means		名資産家
43-1	the contents of her letter		名彼女の手紙の内容
43-2	be content *with* the result		形結果に満足している
44-1	in some respects		名いくつかの点で
44-2	respect the law		動法を尊重する
45-1	the ability to reason		動推理する能力
45-2	He lost all reason.		名彼はすっかり理性を失った
46-1	the cause of the failure		名失敗の原因
46-2	cause a lot of trouble		動多くの問題を引き起こす
46-3	advance the cause of peace		名平和運動を推進する

No.	英語フレーズ	フレーズ書きこみ	日本語フレーズ
47-1	hold a meeting		動 会合を開く
47-2	They hold that the earth is flat.		動 彼らは地球は平らだと考える
48-1	make a fortune in oil		名 石油で財産を築く
48-2	bring *good* fortune		名 幸運をもたらす
49-1	the future of humanity		名 人類の未来
49-2	science and *the* humanities		名 自然科学と人文科学
50	a means to an end		名 目的を果たす手段
51-1	form a new company		動 新しい会社を作る
51-2	*fill out* the application form		名 申込用紙に記入する
51-3	Knowledge is a form *of* power.		名 知識は一種の力だ
52-1	I have no change with me.		名 小銭の持ち合わせがない
52-2	Keep the change.		名 おつりはいりません
53-1	my present address		形 現在の住所
53-2	*the* present and future		名 現在と未来
53-3	the people present		形 出席している人々
53-4	present a plan *to* the president		動 社長に計画を提示する
53-5	present Mr. Boyd *to* you		動 君にボイド氏を紹介する
53-6	present the winner *with* the prize		動 勝者に賞を与える
54-1	works of art		名 芸術作品
54-2	This plan will work.		動 この計画はうまく行く
55-1	One thing leads *to* another.		動 ひとつの事が別の事を引き起こす
55-2	lead a happy *life*		動 幸福な生活を送る
55-3	leading artists		形 一流のアーティスト
56	There is no life on the moon.		名 月には生物がいない
57-1	I *don't* care what you say.		動 君が何と言おうと気にしない
57-2	A baby requires constant care.		名 赤ちゃんはつねに世話が必要だ
58-1	middle-class families		名 中流階級の家庭
58-2	sleep *in* class		名 授業中にいねむりする
59	his natural abilities		形 彼の生まれながらの才能

No.	英語フレーズ	フレーズ書きこみ	日本語フレーズ
60-1	a life free *from* stress		形 ストレスの無い生活
60-2	free them *from* work		動 彼らを労働から解放する
61-1	head straight *for* Paris		動 まっすぐパリに向かう
61-2	a team headed by a woman		動 女性に率いられたチーム
62-1	deal *with* the problem		動 問題を処理する
62-2	*a great* deal of data		名 大量のデータ
62-3	*make* a deal *with* Microsoft		名 マイクロソフトと取引する
63-1	my view *of* education		名 教育に関する私の見解
63-2	view Japan *as* a safe society		動 日本を安全な社会と考える
64	the chance *of* making them angry		名 彼らを怒らせる可能性
65-1	very close *to* the city		形 都市にとても近い
65-2	a close friend		形 親しい友達
65-3	a close examination		形 綿密な検査
66-1	protect workers' interests		名 労働者の利益を守る
66-2	lend money at high interest rates		名 高い利率で金を貸す
67	fail *to* understand him		動 彼を理解できない
68-1	a major problem		形 主要な問題
68-2	major *in* economics		動 経済学を専攻する
69-1	agree *to* his proposal		動 彼の提案に同意する
69-2	I agree *with* you.		動 私も君と同じ考えである
70-1	British colonial rule		名 イギリスの植民地支配
70-2	Small families are *the* rule in Japan.		名 日本では小家族が普通だ
71-1	the process of thought		名 思考の過程
71-2	how to process meat		動 肉を加工する方法
71-3	process data with a computer		動 コンピュータでデータを処理する
72-1	a large amount of water		名 大量の水
72-2	The expenses amount *to* $90.		動 経費は合計90ドルになる
72-3	This act amounts *to* stealing.		動 この行為は盗みに等しい
73	long *for* world peace		動 世界平和を切望する

4 多義語

No.	英語フレーズ	フレーズ書きこみ	日本語フレーズ
74-1 ☐	The line is busy.		名 電話が話し中だ
74-2 ☐	wait *in* line		名 1列に並んで待つ
74-3 ☐	*drop* him a line		名 彼に短い手紙を書く
74-4 ☐	this line *of business*		名 こういう種類の仕事
75 ☐	a word of six letters		名 6文字の単語
76-1 ☐	People are subject *to* the law.		形 人は法に支配される
76-2 ☐	I am subject *to* illness.		形 私は病気にかかりやすい
76-3 ☐	Let's change the subject.		名 話題を変えよう
76-4 ☐	My favorite subject is math.		名 好きな学科は数学です
76-5 ☐	the subject of the experiment		名 その実験の被験者
77-1 ☐	*the* rest of his life		名 彼の残りの人生
77-2 ☐	Let's take a rest.		名 休息をとろう
78-1 ☐	the fine *for* speeding		名 スピード違反の罰金
78-2 ☐	be fined $60		動 60ドルの罰金を科される
78-3 ☐	fine sand on the beach		形 海岸の細かい砂
79 ☐	My shoes have worn thin.		動 靴がすり減って薄くなった
80-1 ☐	Please remember me *to* your wife.		動 奥さんによろしく伝えてください
80-2 ☐	remember *to* lock the door		動 忘れずにドアにカギをかける
81-1 ☐	The insurance covers the cost.		動 保険で費用をまかなう
81-2 ☐	cover the big news		動 大ニュースを報道[取材]する
81-3 ☐	cover 120 miles an hour		動 1時間に120マイル進む
82 ☐	book a flight		動 飛行機を予約する
83 ☐	store information in a computer		動 コンピュータに情報を蓄える
84-1 ☐	save money for a new house		動 新しい家のためお金を蓄える
84-2 ☐	save time and trouble		動 時間と手間を省く
84-3 ☐	answer all the questions save one		前 1つを除きすべての質問に答える
85-1 ☐	serve good food		動 うまい料理を出す
85-2 ☐	serve many purposes		動 多くの目的に役立つ
85-3 ☐	serve the king		動 王に仕える

No.	英語フレーズ	フレーズ書きこみ	日本語フレーズ
86-1	Black people account *for* 10% of the population.		動黒人が人口の10%を占める
86-2	This accounts *for* the failure.		動これが失敗の原因だ
86-3	account *for* the difference		動違いを説明する
87	the art of writing		名書く技術
88-1	He was fired *from* his job.		動彼は仕事をクビになった
88-2	fire into the crowd		動群衆に向かって発砲する
89-1	a strange flying object		名奇妙な飛行物体
89-2	an object of study		名研究の対象
89-3	object *to* his drink*ing*		動彼が酒を飲むのに反対する
90-1	manage *to* catch the train		動なんとか列車に間に合う
90-2	manage a big company		動大会社を経営する
91	*On* what grounds do you say that?		名どんな根拠でそう言うのか
92-1	assume that money can buy happiness		動金で幸福が買えると思い込む
92-2	assume responsibility		動責任を引き受ける
93-1	direct contact		形直接の接触
93-2	direct his attention *to* the fact		動その事実に彼の注意を向ける
93-3	direct her *to* the station		動彼女に駅への道を教える
93-4	direct the workers		動労働者たちに指図する
94-1	If he fails, it'll be *my* fault.		名彼が失敗したら私の責任だ
94-2	He has a lot of faults.		名彼は欠点が多い
95-1	He is tired due *to* lack of sleep.		形彼は睡眠不足のせいで疲れている
95-2	pay due respect		形十分な敬意を払う
95-3	The train is due *to* arrive at ten.		形その列車は10時に着く予定だ
95-4	The report is due next Wednesday.		形レポートは水曜が期限だ
96-1	*in* a scientific manner		名科学的な方法で
96-2	her friendly manner		名彼女の好意的な態度
96-3	It's bad manners to spit.		名つばを吐くのは行儀が悪い
97	a pretty long time		副かなり長い間

No.	英語フレーズ	フレーズ書きこみ	日本語フレーズ
98-1	The man struck me *as* strange.		動 その男は私に奇妙な印象を与えた
98-2	Suddenly an idea struck him.		動 突然彼にある考えが浮かんだ
98-3	The typhoon struck Osaka.		動 その台風は大阪を襲った
99-1	*get* regular exercise		名 規則的に運動する
99-2	exercise power over people		動 人々に対し権力を用いる
100-1	maintain health		動 健康を維持する
100-2	maintain that he is innocent		動 彼の無罪を主張する
101-1	work for a big firm		名 大きな会社に勤める
101-2	a firm belief		形 堅い信念
102-1	a newspaper article		名 新聞の記事
102-2	an article for sale		名 販売用の品物
103	That's what counts.		動 それが重要なことだ
104-1	appreciate his talent		動 彼の才能を高く評価する
104-2	appreciate music		動 音楽を鑑賞する
104-3	I appreciate your help.		動 君の助けに感謝する
105-1	take strong measures		名 強硬な手段を用いる
105-2	a measure of respect		名 ある程度の尊敬
106-1	have a good command of English		名 英語をうまくあやつる能力がある
106-2	The hill commands a fine view.		動 丘からいい景色を見わたせる
106-3	command great respect		動 大いに尊敬を集める
107-1	bear the pain		動 痛みに耐える
107-2	bear a child		動 子供を産む
107-3	bear relation to the matter		動 その問題に関係を持つ
108-1	stick *to* the schedule		動 予定を守る
108-2	get stuck on a crowded train		動 混んだ列車で動けなくなる
108-3	stick out the tongue		動 舌を突き出す
108-4	The song stuck in my mind.		動 その歌は私の心に残った
109-1	a fixed point		動 固定された点
109-2	fix a broken car		動 壊れた車を修理する
109-3	I'll fix you a drink.		動 飲み物を作ってあげる

No.	英語フレーズ	フレーズ書きこみ	日本語フレーズ
110-1	*in* a similar fashion		名 同じようなやり方で
110-2	fashion a new world		動 新しい世界を作る
111-1	free of charge		名 料金不要で
111-2	charge a high price		動 高い代金を請求する
111-3	He is *in* charge *of* the case.		名 彼がその事件の担当だ
111-4	be charged *with* murder		動 殺人で告訴される
112-1	observe the comet		動 彗星を観察する
112-2	observe that prices would fall		動 物価は下がると述べる
112-3	observe the rule		動 規則を守る
113-1	conduct an experiment		動 実験を行う
113-2	the standards of conduct		名 行動の基準
113-3	conduct electricity		動 電気を伝える
114-1	I'll keep *my* word.		名 私は約束を守る
114-2	Could I *have a* word *with* you?		名 ちょっと話があるんですが
115-1	*get in* touch *with* him by phone		名 電話で彼に連絡をとる
115-2	The story touched him deeply.		動 その話は彼を深く感動させた
115-3	add *a* touch *of* spice		名 スパイスを少し加える
116-1	agree *to* some degree		名 ある程度まで同意する
116-2	get a master's degree		名 修士の学位を取る
117	learn a lesson from the failure		名 失敗から教訓を学ぶ
118-1	deny the existence of God		動 神の存在を否定する
118-2	deny them their civil rights		動 彼らに市民権を与えない
119	take a break for a cup of tea		名 一休みしてお茶を飲む
120	the nature of language		名 言語の本質
121-1	a letter addressed to him		動 彼に宛てられた手紙
121-2	address climate change		動 気候変動に取り組む
121-3	address the audience		動 聴衆に呼びかける
121-4	the opening address		名 開会の演説
122-1	the freedom of *the* press		名 出版の自由
122-2	be pressed for time		動 時間が切迫している

4

多義語

No.	英語フレーズ	フレーズ書きこみ	日本語フレーズ
123-1	an expensive item		名高価な品物
123-2	the top news item		名トップニュースの記事
124-1	feel pity *for* the victims		名犠牲者に同情する
124-2	It's *a* pity that he can't come.		名彼が来られないのは残念なことだ
125	beat the champion		動チャンピオンに勝つ
126-1	point *out* that it is wrong		動それは誤りだと指摘する
126-2	There's no point *in* writing it.		名それを書く意味はない
126-3	prove his point		名彼の主張を証明する
127-1	I lived there once.		副私はかつてそこに住んでいた
127-2	Once she arrives, we can start.		接彼女が来るとすぐ我々は出発できる
128-1	a healthy diet		名健康的な食事
128-2	She is *on* a diet.		名彼女は食事制限をしている
128-3	a member of *the* Diet		名国会議員
129	write a paper on economics		名経済学の論文を書く
130-1	cash a check		名小切手を現金に換える
130-2	a dinner check		名ディナーの勘定書
130-3	check bags at the airport		動空港でバッグを預ける
131	Meg is a bright girl.		形メグは賢い子だ
132-1	a sort of bird		名一種の鳥
132-2	sort papers by date		動日付で書類を分類する
133	The case went to court.		名その事件は裁判になった
134-1	He *is* bound *to* fail.		形彼はきっと失敗する
134-2	The plane *is* bound *for* Guam.		形その飛行機はグアム行きだ
134-3	be bound by the law		動法律に縛られる
135-1	a flat surface		形平らな表面
135-2	live in a flat in London		名ロンドンのアパートに住む
136-1	have no spare money		形余分なお金はない
136-2	spare him a few minutes		動彼のために少し時間を割く
136-3	spare him the trouble		動彼の面倒を省く
136-4	spare *no* effort to help her		動彼女を助ける努力を惜しまない

No.	英語フレーズ	フレーズ書きこみ	日本語フレーズ
137-1	the capital of Australia		名オーストラリアの首都
137-2	labor and capital		名労働と資本
138	speak in a foreign tongue		名外国の言葉でしゃべる
139	credit for the discovery		名その発見の功績
140	succeed *to* the crown		動王位を受け継ぐ
141-1	settle the dispute		動紛争を解決する
141-2	settle in America		動アメリカに定住する
141-3	get married and settle *down*		動結婚して落ち着く
142-1	a vision of the city		名その都市の未来像
142-2	a leader of vision		名先見の明のある指導者
142-3	have poor vision		名視力が弱い
143-1	I have but one question.		副1つだけ質問がある
143-2	They *all* went out but me.		前私を除いて皆出かけた
144-1	in a given situation		形ある特定の状況で
144-2	given the present conditions		前現状を考慮すると
144-3	given *that* you are young		接君が若いことを考慮すると
145-1	equal pay for equal work		名同じ仕事に対する同じ給料
145-2	Honesty doesn't always pay.		動正直は割に合うとは限らない
146-1	*a* good many people		形かなり多くの人
146-2	work for the public good		名公共の利益のために働く
147-1	teach students discipline		名学生に規律を教える
147-2	scientists of many disciplines		名いろんな分野の科学者たち
148-1	an electricity bill		名電気代の請求書
148-2	a ten dollar bill		名10ドル紙幣
148-3	pass a bill		名法案を可決する
149-1	breathe a sigh of relief		名安心してため息をつく
149-2	relief from poverty		名貧困に対する救済
149-3	relief from stress		名ストレスの除去

No.	英語フレーズ	フレーズ書きこみ	日本語フレーズ
150-1	board a plane		動飛行機に乗り込む
150-2	the school board		名教育委員会
151	She *got* mad at me.		形彼女は私に腹を立てた
152-1	yield food and wood		動食料や木材を産出する
152-2	yield *to* pressure		動圧力に屈する
152-3	Radio yielded *to* television.		動ラジオはテレビに取って代わられた
153-1	a rear seat		名後部座席
153-2	rear three children		動3人の子供を育てる
154-1	fancy restaurant		形高級レストラン
154-2	fancy myself a novelist		動自分が小説家だと想像する
155-1	feel no shame		名恥と思わない
155-2	What *a* shame!		名なんと残念なことか
156-1	waste money		動お金を浪費する
156-2	industrial waste		名産業廃棄物
157-1	drive the dog *away*		動犬を追い払う
157-2	be driven by curiosity		動好奇心に駆りたてられる
157-3	my strong drive to succeed		名成功したいという強い欲求
158	English with an Italian accent		名イタリアなまりの英語
159	He will make a good teacher.		動彼はよい教師になるだろう
160-1	in his late thirties		形彼の30代の終わりごろに
160-2	*the* late Mr. Ford		形故フォード氏
161-1	her body and soul		名彼女の肉体と魂
161-2	There was *not a* soul there.		名そこには1人もいなかった
162	arms control		名軍備制限
163-1	virtue and vice		名美徳と悪徳
163-2	vice president		形副大統領
164	a five-story building		名5階建ての建物
165	She was moved by my story.		動彼女は私の話に感動した
166	a parking lot		名駐車場

No.	英語フレーズ	フレーズ書きこみ	日本語フレーズ
167-1	teach the dolphin new tricks		名 イルカに新しい芸を教える
167-2	a trick for memorizing words		名 単語を覚えるコツ
167-3	*play* a trick *on* the teacher		名 先生にいたずらする
167-4	trick him *into* buying the pot		動 彼をだましてそのつぼを買わせる
167-5	a clever trick		名 巧妙なたくらみ
168	New companies will spring up there.		動 そこに新しい会社が出現するだろう
169-1	pose a problem		動 問題を引き起こす
169-2	pose a question		動 疑問を提起する
170-1	The water is fit *to* drink.		形 その水は飲むのに適する
170-2	go to the gym to keep fit		形 健康でいるためにジムに通う
171-1	take notes on what you hear		名 聞くことをメモする
171-2	He noted that America is a big country.		動 アメリカは大国だと彼は書いた
171-3	Note that the book is non-fiction.		動 その本は実話だということに注意しなさい
171-4	He is noted *for* his intelligence.		形 彼は知的なことで有名だ
171-5	a ten-pound note		名 10ポンド紙幣
172-1	gun control laws		名 銃規制法
172-2	control group		名 実験の対照群
173-1	the school authorities		名 学校当局
173-2	the authority of the state		名 国家の権力
173-3	an authority *on* biology		名 生物学の権威
174-1	Consider a fruit, say, an orange.		フルーツ, たとえばオレンジを考えよ
174-2	Let's say you have a million dollars.		君が100万ドル持っていると仮定しよう
174-3	What do you say to go*ing* on a trip?		旅に出かけたらどうですか

4

多義語

ジャンル別英単語

"Words cut more than swords."

* * *

言葉は剣よりも切れる。

● 職業　ジャンル別 ①　(p. 108)

No.	単語	意味	書きこみ①	書きこみ②	書きこみ③
1	**accountant** [əkáuntənt]	会計士			
2	**attendant** [əténdənt]	接客係			
3	**barber** [bάəbə]	理髪師			
4	**butcher** [bútʃə]	肉屋			
5	**carpenter** [kάəpntə]	大工			
6	**cashier** [kæʃíə]	レジ係			
7	**chairman** [tʃéərmən]	議長			
8	**dentist** [déntəst]	歯科医			
9	**director** [diréktə]	管理者			
10	**expert** [ékspəːrt]	専門家			
11	**fisherman** [fíʃəmən]	漁師			
12	**grocer** [gróusər]	食料雑貨商			
13	**housewife** [háuswaif]	主婦			
14	**president** [prézidənt]	大統領			
15	**professor** [prəfésər]	教授			
16	**soldier** [sóuldʒər]	兵士			

● 人間関係　ジャンル別 ②　(p. 108)

No.	単語	意味	書きこみ①	書きこみ②	書きこみ③
1	**boss** [bɔ́(ː)s]	上司			
2	**coworker** [kóuwərkər]	同僚			
3	**dad** [dǽd]	とうさん			
4	**grandchild** [grǽntʃaild]	孫			
5	**grand-parents** [grǽnpeərənts]	祖父母			
6	**kinship** [kínʃip]	親類関係			
7	**Majesty** [mǽdʒəsti]	陛下			
8	**marital** [mǽərətl]	夫婦の			

9 □	**mom** [mám]	かあさん			
10 □	**sir** [sə́:r]	お客様			
11 □	**spouse** [spáus]	配偶者			

● 野菜・果物　ジャンル別 3 (p. 170)

No.	単語	意味	書きこみ①	書きこみ②	書きこみ③
1 □	**bean** [bíːn]	豆(科の植物)			
2 □	**cabbage** [kǽbidʒ]	キャベツ			
3 □	**cucumber** [kjúːkʌmbər]	キュウリ			
4 □	**egg plant** [éɡ plǽnt]	ナス			
5 □	**garlic** [gáːrlik]	ニンニク			
6 □	**ginger** [dʒíndʒər]	ショウガ			
7 □	**lettuce** [létəs]	レタス			
8 □	**pea** [píː]	(さや)エンドウ			
9 □	**pear** [péər]	洋ナシ			
10 □	**spinach** [spínitʃ]	ホウレン草			
11 □	**squash** [skwáʃ]	カボチャ			

● 天 気　ジャンル別 4 (p. 175)

No.	単語	意味	書きこみ①	書きこみ②	書きこみ③
1 □	**fog** [fɔ́(ː)g]	霧			
2 □	**frost** [frɔ́(ː)st]	霜			
3 □	**hail** [héil]	あられ			
4 □	**mist** [míst]	かすみ			
5 □	**shower** [ʃáuər]	にわか雨			
6 □	**thunder** [θʌ́ndər]	雷鳴			
7 □	**thunderstorm** [θʌ́ndərstɔəm]	激しい雷雨			
8 □	**tornado** [tɔənéidou]	竜巻			
9 □	**twilight** [twáilait]	夕方			

★

ジャンル別

● 動物　ジャンル別 5 (p. 176)

No.	単語	意味	書きこみ①	書きこみ②	書きこみ③
1	**animal** [ǽnəml]	動物			
2	**bat** [bǽt]	コウモリ			
3	**bull** [búl]	雄牛			
4	**camel** [kǽml]	ラクダ			
5	**cow** [káu]	乳牛			
6	**deer** [díər]	シカ			
7	**donkey** [dáŋki]	ロバ			
8	**elephant** [éləfənt]	ゾウ			
9	**fox** [fáks]	キツネ			
10	**giraffe** [dʒərǽf]	キリン			
11	**goat** [góut]	ヤギ			
12	**hare** [héər]	ノウサギ			
13	**hippopotamus** [hipəpútəməs]	カバ			
14	**kitten** [kítn]	子ネコ			
15	**leopard** [lépərd]	ヒョウ			
16	**lizard** [lízərd]	トカゲ			
17	**mole** [móul]	モグラ			
18	**mouse** [máus]	ハツカネズミ			
19	**ox** [áks]	雄牛			
20	**puppy** [pʌ́pi]	子犬			
21	**rabbit** [rǽbət]	ウサギ			
22	**rat** [rǽt]	ドブネズミ			
23	**reindeer** [réindiər]	トナカイ			
24	**rhinoceros** [rainásərəs]	サイ			
25	**sea lion** [síː láiən]	アシカ			
26	**seal** [síːl]	アザラシ			
27	**sheep** [ʃíːp]	ヒツジ			

158

28 ☐	**snake** [snéik]	ヘビ			
29 ☐	**squirrel** [skwə́:rəl]	リス			
30 ☐	**turtle** [tə́:rtl]	カメ			
31 ☐	**wild boar** [wáild bɔ́:r]	イノシシ			
32 ☐	**wolf** [wúlf]	オオカミ			
33 ☐	**zebra** [zí:brə]	シマウマ			

● 植 物　　ジャンル別 ⑥ (p. 187)

No.	単語	意味	書きこみ①	書きこみ②	書きこみ③
1 ☐	**bamboo** [bæmbú:]	竹			
2 ☐	**cactus** [kǽktəs]	サボテン			
3 ☐	**cedar** [sí:də]	スギ			
4 ☐	**chestnut** [tʃésnʌt]	クリ(の木)			
5 ☐	**grass** [grǽs]	草			
6 ☐	**ivy** [áivi]	ツタ			
7 ☐	**leaf** [lí:f]	葉			
8 ☐	**lily** [líli]	ユリ			
9 ☐	**maple** [méipl]	カエデ			
10 ☐	**moss** [mɔ́:s]	コケ			
11 ☐	**oak** [óuk]	オーク			
12 ☐	**palm** [pá:m]	ヤシ			
13 ☐	**pine** [páin]	マツ			
14 ☐	**redwood** [rédwud]	セコイア			
15 ☐	**seaweed** [sí:wi:d]	海藻			
16 ☐	**walnut** [wɔ́:lnʌt]	クルミ(の木)			
17 ☐	**weed** [wí:d]	雑草			
18 ☐	**willow** [wílou]	柳			

★
ジャンル別

● 虫　ジャンル別 7 (p. 216)

No.	単語	意味	書きこみ①	書きこみ②	書きこみ③
1	**ant** [ǽnt]	アリ			
2	**bee** [bíː]	ハチ			
3	**beetle** [bíːtl]	カブトムシ			
4	**bug** [bʌ́g]	虫			
5	**butterfly** [bʌ́tərflai]	チョウ			
6	**caterpillar** [kǽtərpilər]	イモムシ			
7	**cicada** [səkéidə]	セミ			
8	**cockroach** [kákroutʃ]	ゴキブリ			
9	**flea** [flíː]	ノミ			
10	**fly** [flái]	ハエ			
11	**mosquito** [məskíːtou]	カ			
12	**moth** [mɔ́(ː)θ]	ガ			
13	**snail** [snéil]	カタツムリ			
14	**spider** [spáidər]	クモ			
15	**wasp** [wάːsp]	ジガバチ			
16	**worm** [wə́ːrm]	イモムシ			

● 鳥　ジャンル別 8 (p. 216)

No.	単語	意味	書きこみ①	書きこみ②	書きこみ③
1	**canary** [kənéəri]	カナリア			
2	**crow** [króu]	カラス			
3	**cuckoo** [kúːkuː]	カッコウ			
4	**dove** [dʌ́v]	ハト			
5	**duck** [dʌ́k]	アヒル			
6	**eagle** [íːgl]	ワシ			
7	**goose** [gúːs]	ガチョウ			
8	**gull** [gʌ́l]	カモメ			

160

No.	単語	意味	書きこみ①	書きこみ②	書きこみ③
9	**hawk** [hɔ́:k]	タカ			
10	**hen** [hén]	めんどり			
11	**owl** [ául]	フクロウ			
12	**parrot** [pǽrət]	オウム			
13	**peacock** [pí:kɑk]	クジャク			
14	**pigeon** [pídʒən]	ハト			
15	**robin** [rάbin]	コマドリ			
16	**sparrow** [spǽərou]	スズメ			
17	**swallow** [swάlou]	ツバメ			
18	**turkey** [tə́:rki]	七面鳥			

● 図 形　　ジャンル別 9　(p. 297)

No.	単語	意味	書きこみ①	書きこみ②	書きこみ③
1	**angle** [ǽŋgl]	角			
2	**circle** [sə́:rkl]	円			
3	**cone** [kóun]	円すい			
4	**cube** [kjú:b]	立方体			
5	**oval** [óuvl]	卵形(の)			
6	**pentagon** [péntəgan]	5角形			
7	**plane** [pléin]	面			
8	**rectangle** [réktæŋgl]	長方形			
9	**side** [sáid]	辺			
10	**square** [skwéər]	正方形			
11	**triangle** [tráiæŋgl]	3角形			

★ ジャンル別

● 食事　ジャンル別 10 (p. 308)

No.	単語	意味	書きこみ①	書きこみ②	書きこみ③
1	**chopsticks** [tʃápstiks]	はし			
2	**dessert** [dizə́:rt]	デザート			
3	**dish** [díʃ]	皿			
4	**kettle** [kétl]	やかん			
5	**lid** [líd]	ふた			
6	**mug** [mʌ́g]	マグカップ			
7	**plate** [pléit]	取り皿			
8	**sauser** [sɔ́:sər]	受け皿			
9	**steak** [stéik]	ステーキ			
10	**stew** [stʃú:]	シチュー			

● 海の生き物　ジャンル別 11 (p. 310)

No.	単語	意味	書きこみ①	書きこみ②	書きこみ③
1	**a school of fish**	魚の群れ			
2	**cod** [káːd]	タラ			
3	**dolphin** [dɑ́lfin]	イルカ			
4	**jelly fish** [dʒéli fíʃ]	クラゲ			
5	**octopus** [ɑ́ktəpəs]	タコ			
6	**oyster** [ɔ́istər]	カキ			
7	**salmon** [sǽmən]	サケ			
8	**sardine** [sɑːrdíːn]	イワシ			
9	**shark** [ʃɑ́ːrk]	サメ			
10	**shell** [ʃél]	貝			
11	**squid** [skwíd]	イカ			
12	**trout** [tráut]	マス			
13	**tuna** [tʃúːnə]	マグロ			
14	**whale** [hwéil]	クジラ			

162

● 人体　　ジャンル別 12　(p. 311)

No.	単語	意味	書きこみ①	書きこみ②	書きこみ③
1	**ankle** [ǽŋkl]	足首			
2	**beard** [bíərd]	あごひげ			
3	**bone** [bóun]	骨			
4	**bowel** [bául]	腸			
5	**breast** [brést]	胸			
6	**brow** [bráu]	額^{ひたい}			
7	**cheek** [tʃíːk]	ほお			
8	**chest** [tʃést]	胸			
9	**cortex** [kɔ́ːrteks]	皮質			
10	**elbow** [élbou]	ひじ			
11	**forehead** [fɔ́(ː)rəd]	額^{ひたい}			
12	**jaw** [dʒɔ́ː]	あご			
13	**kidney** [kídni]	腎臓			
14	**knee** [níː]	ひざ			
15	**liver** [lívər]	肝臓			
16	**shoulder** [ʃóuldər]	肩			
17	**skeleton** [skélətn]	骨格			
18	**skin** [skín]	はだ			
19	**stomach** [stʌ́mək]	腹部			
20	**throat** [θróut]	のど			
21	**toe** [tóu]	足の指			
22	**tooth** [túːθ]	歯			
23	**wrinkle** [ríŋkl]	しわ			

★

ジャンル別

● 衣服　ジャンル別 13 (p. 311)

No.	単語	意味	書きこみ①	書きこみ②	書きこみ③
1	**blanket** [blǽŋkət]	毛布			
2	**collar** [kálər]	えり			
3	**cosmetics** [kɑzmétiks]	化粧品			
4	**cotton** [kátn]	綿			
5	**dye** [dái]	染料			
6	**feather** [féðər]	羽毛			
7	**fur** [fə́:r]	毛皮			
8	**leather** [léðər]	革			
9	**lipstick** [lípstìk]	口紅			
10	**pants** [pǽnts]	ズボン			
11	**razor** [réizər]	かみそり			
12	**silk** [sílk]	絹			
13	**wool** [wúl]	羊毛			

● 公共施設・建物　ジャンル別 14 (p. 312)

No.	単語	意味	書きこみ①	書きこみ②	書きこみ③
1	**aquarium** [əkwéəriəm]	水族館			
2	**bank** [bǽŋk]	銀行			
3	**botanical garden** [bətǽnikl gá:rdn]	植物園			
4	**church** [tʃə́:rtʃ]	教会			
5	**college** [kálidʒ]	(単科)大学			
6	**dormitory** [dɔ́:rmətɔ:ri]	寮			
7	**factory** [fǽktəri]	工場			
8	**gallery** [gǽləri]	美術館			
9	**garage** [gərá:dʒ]	車庫			
10	**hall** [hɔ́:l]	会館			
11	**hospital** [háspitl]	病院			

No.	単語	意味	書きこみ①	書きこみ②	書きこみ③
12	**museum** [mju:zíəm]	博物館			
13	**palace** [pǽləs]	宮殿			
14	**park** [páːrk]	公園			
15	**restaurant** [réstərənt]	レストラン			
16	**theater** [θíətər]	劇場			
17	**university** [juːnəvóːrsəti]	(総合)大学			

● 住居　ジャンル別 15 (p. 312)

No.	単語	意味	書きこみ①	書きこみ②	書きこみ③
1	**apartment** [əpáːrtmənt]	アパート			
2	**backyard** [bǽkjáːrd]	裏庭			
3	**ceiling** [síːliŋ]	天井			
4	**chamber** [tʃéimbər]	小部屋			
5	**closet** [klázət]	クロゼット			
6	**corridor** [kɔ́(ː)rədər]	ろうか			
7	**downstairs** [daunstéərz]	階下			
8	**drawer** [drɔ́ːr]	引き出し			
9	**elevator** [éləveitər]	エレベーター			
10	**escalator** [éskəleitər]	エスカレーター			
11	**gate** [géit]	門			
12	**rail** [réil]	手すり			
13	**roof** [rúːf]	屋根			
14	**stairs** [stéərz]	階段			
15	**study** [stʌ́di]	書斎			
16	**upstairs** [ʌpstéərz]	階上			
17	**wall** [wɔ́ːl]	壁			
18	**yard** [jáːrd]	庭			

ジャンル別

● 教育　　ジャンル別 16　(p. 345)

No.	単語	意味	書きこみ①	書きこみ②	書きこみ③
1	**admission** [ədmíʃən]	入学			
2	**applicant** [ǽplikənt]	志願者			
3	**bachelor** [bǽtʃələr]	学士			
4	**credit** [krédit]	単位			
5	**curriculum** [kəríkjələm]	カリキュラム			
6	**degree** [digríː]	学位			
7	**department** [dipáːrtmənt]	学部			
8	**diploma** [diplóumə]	卒業証書			
9	**dorm** [dɔ́ːrm]	寮			
10	**enrollment** [enróulmənt]	入学			
11	**freshman** [fréʃmən]	新入生			
12	**graduate** [grǽdʒuət]	大学卒業生			
13	**handout** [hǽndaut]	プリント			
14	**lecture** [léktʃər]	講義			
15	**major** [méidʒer]	専攻			
16	**material** [mətíəriəl]	資料			
17	**office hours**	研究室在室時間			
18	**photocopy** [fóutoukɑpi]	コピー			
19	**qualified** [kwɑ́ləfàid]	資格のある			
20	**quiz** [kwíz]	小テスト			
21	**recommendation** [rekəməndéiʃən]	推薦(状)			
22	**requirement** [rikwáiərmənt]	必要条件			
23	**scholarship** [skɑ́lərʃip]	奨学金			
24	**semester** [səméstər]	学期			
25	**sophomore** [sɑ́fəmɔːr]	2年生			
26	**syllabus** [síləbəs]	シラバス			
27	**term** [tə́ːrm]	学期			

28 ☐	**tuition** [tjuː(ː)íʃən]	授業(料)			
29 ☐	**tutor** [tjúːtər]	個別指導教員			
30 ☐	**undergraduate** [ʌndərgrǽdʒuət]	大学生			

システム英単語 Basic〈5訂版対応〉

フレーズ・単語書きこみワークブック

著　　者	霜　　康　司
	刀祢　雅　彦
発　行　者	山﨑　良　子
印刷・製本	日 経 印 刷 株 式 会 社
発　行　所	駿 台 文 庫 株 式 会 社

〒101-0062　東京都千代田区神田駿河台1-7-4
小畑ビル内
TEL. 編集 03(5259)3302
販売 03(5259)3301
《④ - 168pp.》

ISBN978-4-7961-1144-7　　　　Printed in Japan

駿台文庫 Web サイト
https://www.sundaibunko.jp